'Out of Darkness into His Marvellous Light'

(1 Peter 2:9)

Malcolm & Margaret Wilson

To Jean & Barrie, with love & best wishes Malcolm Margaret xx

Marvellous Light Ministries

Bible quotations are from the New King James Bible unless otherwise stated.

Hebrew/Greek Translations are from Zodhiates Hebrew Greek Study Bible.

ISBN: 1 874367 68 X

Names have been changed where necessary to protect the identity of persons in this book.

The authors may be contacted in the UK at:

Marvellous Light Ministries
PO Box 28
Camberley
Surrey GU17 0RF

Fax: 01276 36213
e-mail address: 106372,3070@compuserve.com

and in the USA at:

Marvellous Light Ministries
PO Box No. 2512
Myrtle Beach
SC 29277

Typeset by CRB Associates, Reepham, Norfolk
Printed in England by Clays Ltd, St Ives plc

Contents

Foreword

by Bishop and Mrs John Stanley

Part One of Malcolm and Margaret Wilson's book, *Out of Darkness into His Marvellous Light*, gives a dramatic insight into the works of darkness.

The lure of psychic answers caught Malcolm in the web of demonic powers but he found salvation and deliverance in Jesus Christ of Nazareth. Like Malcolm's ancestor, Professor Sir James Young Simpson, physician to rich and poor, Malcolm is compelled to bring the truth and lessons he has learned to a hurting world. Malcolm's life is a testimony to the fact that sin and its pain is removed by the blood of Jesus.

As a Spirit-filled Christian at the age of ten, Margaret's story is different. She brushed close to darkness when she went her own way as a teenager and young woman. Yet God's faithfulness brought her back into the Light and then brought Malcolm into her life that they might journey in the Light together. The principles of salvation, healing and deliverance are ably set forth in their story.

Part Two is a call for believers to be ready for what is to come. The Time Formula in 2 Peter 3:8 is in perfect keeping with what science has found in God's consistent universe. The constancy of the speed of light is a totally reliable factor in nature. On this we can rely, *'God is light, and in Him is no darkness at all'* (1 John 1:5). We, as children of light will soon have a body suited to move naturally in the realm of light speed. By God's grace we now have the scientific understanding to comprehend **Peter's Time Formula**. Blessings and thanks to Malcolm and Margaret for laying it all out so clearly.

The inclusion of Tommy Hick's prophecy in 1961 gives an emphatic exclamation point and a resounding Amen to what Malcolm and Margaret have conveyed. We also have had many revelations that are in perfect alignment with all this book presents.

We highly recommend this book to all the end-time generation and as a witness to those caught in darkness that they too may come into His Marvellous Light.

Bishop and Mrs John Stanley
Vashon Island, Washington, USA
17 August, 1997

✣   ✣   ✣

We are extremely grateful to Bishop and Mrs John Stanley for writing the foreword to our book. Although Bishop John Stanley is known throughout the world, his name may not be familiar to some. We thought it useful therefore, to give the reader some information on his background and achievements.

Malcolm and Margaret Wilson

Bishop John M. Stanley DD, OSJ

Metropolitan John M. Stanley is Exarch (Apostolikos) of the Orthodox Church of the East, a part of the ancient church, established in Jerusalem on the Day of Pentecost. His roots trace back to the church founded in India by St Thomas the Apostle. He is a Grand Prelate of justice of the Orthodox Knight Hospitallers, the Sovereign Order of St John of Jerusalem, with its 1000-year history of bringing medical care for the poor in Europe and the world.

He studied at Seattle Pacific University, University of Washington, Northwest Biblical Seminary, St Thomas Theological School, and Seattle University. He did doctoral graduate studies in psychology at St Thomas and additional graduate work at SU, SPU and NBS.

He has worked closely with the FGBMFI as an international speaker since 1963. He was involved in airlifts to London as well as airlifts to Honduras, India, Japan, Korea, Taiwan and Vietnam. The founder of the FGBMFI, Demos Shakarian, referred to Bishop Stanley as 'his prophet'. Bishop Stanley has written a book on the work of the FGBMFI.

He has ministered the Gospel throughout the world and met with leaders in Israel, Egypt, India and Pakistan. In recognition of almost forty years as an international leader for peace, Bishop Stanley received the Gold Angel Award for International Peace in 1990. He is a prominent member of many important organisations too numerous to list here but some of these include:

President – World Alliance for Peace
Director of Spirituality – Southern California Ecumenical Conference
Director of Education – National Welfare Foundation, Pakistan
Vice President – World Fellowship of Religions
Chaplain – International Order of St Luke

Introduction

Malcolm and Margaret Wilson are just two ordinary people, implicit believers in the Gospel of the Lord Jesus Christ. They are members of the King's Church, Aldershot, England, where they fulfilled a minor pastoral leadership role, until they established **'Marvellous Light Ministries'** in order to follow the call that they believe God has made on their lives. They have ministered in churches and meetings both in the USA and England. The Lord has blessed Malcolm and Margaret's ministry with amazing signs and wonders as people have been dramatically saved, healed and delivered through the power of the Holy Spirit.

In this book they have recorded their testimonies, their feelings, their thoughts and their experience of the Spirit-filled Christian life, as far as possible, taking great care to ensure that every detail of their testimonies is true and accurate.

Malcolm is a member of the Guildford, England, chapter of the **Full Gospel Businessmen's Fellowship International**, and former Coca-Cola National Retail Sales Manager (England and Wales).

Malcolm, who was saved in 1989 at the age of forty-two, declares:

> 'I was on the way to the top of my career when a series of extraordinary events caused my life as a high-flying business executive to fall apart. I then set off down a path to destruction, turning to the occult and Spiritism for answers, only to find myself in even deeper trouble.

The road to damnation stretched before me, when God sovereignly moved and snatched me from the fire. My sinful life was in an awful mess, I had no hope, I deserved nothing but judgement. Instead,

> "... [Jesus] *heard my cry.*
> *He also brought me up out of a horrible pit,*
> *Out of the miry clay,*
> *And set my feet upon a rock,*
> *And established my steps.*
> *He has put a new song in my mouth –*
> *Praise to our God;*
> *Many will see it and fear,*
> *And will trust in the* LORD." '   (Psalm 40:1–3)

Margaret, formerly a secretary at Pinewood Film Studios, England says:

> 'I found grace in the wilderness – when desperate circumstances threatened my sanity.'

> *'The* LORD *has appeared of old to me saying:*
> *"Yes, I have loved you with an everlasting love;*
> *Therefore with lovingkindness I have drawn you.*
> *Again I will build you, and you shall be rebuilt,*
> *O virgin of Israel!*
> *You shall again be adorned with your tambourines,*
> *And shall go forth in the dances of those who rejoice." '*
>   (Jeremiah 31:3–4)

They feel their ministry is to share their story with others, especially the sick, the hurting, those in pain and sorrow, the lost and unsaved and those entangled in any form of occult involvement. Their simple message is that of the Gospel:

Jesus Saves, Jesus Heals, Jesus Delivers.

They know that Jesus offers the free gift of life eternal to all *'who believe in their hearts, and confess with their mouths, that He is the risen Son of God.'*

Malcolm and Margaret, in the second part of their book, describe the fresh 'insight and understanding' they believe they have received on the Rapture of the Body of Christ, His Bride, The Church – and His Second Coming as described in the Bible. The Rapture 'Code' or **'Peter's Time Formula'** is central to this new and unique explanation of the fantastic series of events that are soon to unfold on earth, culminating in the 1000-year, Day of the Lord, the destruction of the existing fallen world and the creation of the new heaven and earth. They do not seek to persuade or convert anyone to their views or opinions. They are anxious not to cause alarm, division or ill feeling among their believing brothers and sisters. They believe that time is short and that a final mighty outpouring of God's Holy Spirit during the tribulation soon to come upon the earth, will result in a final worldwide revival and resultant harvest, that will immediately precede the return to the planet of the Lord Jesus Christ. They hope that many will read their account of how Jesus Christ changed their lives forever and that before or even on, that fast approaching 'Great and terrible day of the Lord', many will make their decision for Jesus and take that first tremendous step:

'Out of darkness into His marvellous light.'

PART ONE

'Out of Darkness into His Marvellous Light'

Chapter 1

Some Childhood Memories
by Malcolm

The Wilson Clan

Family Motto
Aut • Pax • Aut • Bellum
(Either Peace or War)

I was born on 28th May 1947, in Aberdeen, Scotland. Unfortunately my mother was ill for several months after my birth, so I was mostly cared for in my earliest days by my sister Pat. My brother John was ten years older than I and obviously I don't remember too much about him at this time. Early memories were happy until I reached the age of four when I had to have an operation to have my tonsils removed. I did not know it at the time, but this proved such a traumatic experience that it was to colour my relationship with my mother, undermine my confidence and result in my general distrust of women for most of my adult life.

Aberdeen, 'The Silver City by the Golden Sands', as the tourist board describes it, is the third largest in Scotland and has a population of about 190,000 people. Situated on the North-East coast of Scotland, it is famous for its shipbuilding industry, papermills, granite quarrying and engineering. The city boasts one of the oldest Universities in the UK, Marischal College, where Alexander Cruden was educated and who published in 1732, *Cruden's Concordance* to the Old and New Testaments. The city became the centre of the British Oil industry, when large oil fields were discovered offshore in the North Sea during the Seventies and was at that time, home for around ten thousand Americans. Winters were long and cold, or at least they seemed that way to me at the time, often with deep snow from December through to April. Two rivers flow through the city, the Dee and the Don and both frequently froze over in winter.

Academically I was average. Good at English, Geography and History. Especially fond of essay writing, but not too hot in the mathematics department. Scottish education at the time did not really allow the individual to develop outside fairly rigid traditions and values. Children were taught to know their place and any display of individuality was soon curbed. The order of the day was, 'Speak when you are spoken to.' Compared to today, discipline was firm and the use of the Scottish Tawse or leather strap applied to the palm of the hand, was liberal. There was no question of challenging any of the mores or beliefs of one's elders and any sign of original thought or resistance to being forced into a mould was thought to be evidence of delinquency. My first introduction to any kind of Bible Teaching was at our local Scottish Presbyterian church where my sister Pat was the Sunday school teacher. I don't remember too much about the doctrine, but it would have probably been of the stern Scottish Presbyterian variety.

My father worked for the Ministry of Agriculture Fisheries and Food and was an inspector of the egg packing stations where egg producers sent their eggs to be graded and checked for quality.

His own father, my grandfather was a bookkeeper with an engineering firm connected with the local shipbuilding industry, where my brother also served his engineering apprenticeship.

My forebears on my father's side have a long history of service both in the Merchant and Royal Navies. My father's brothers continued the Wilson family tradition in the Merchant Navy where they were both ships' engineering officers. During the Napoleonic wars with France, my great-great-great-grandfather in his youth, was a farm-hand living somewhere near Hastings, Sussex. One evening when he was having a quiet drink in the village inn after a hard day in the fields, a Royal Navy 'Press Gang' paid a visit. In those days wary drinkers drank from pewter tankards with glass bottoms, so they could see if any coins had been slipped unseen into their drinks. Woe betide the poor unsuspecting wretch who drank from a mug and failed to notice the coin which had been planted by the recruiting officer. Drinking from such a doctored mug or glass was deemed to be evidence of having 'taken the King's shilling'. Like it or not that meant that you had volunteered for the Royal Navy in His Majesty's Service.

In this way my ancestor was tricked, clubbed over the head and woke up several hours later on board a British man-o'-war making for the South Atlantic. For fifteen years he was at sea and survived various battles and naval engagements with the French. One day his frigate docked at Aberdeen Harbour and seizing his opportunity, he jumped ship and escaped. Eventually he married a local girl and my father's side of my family were a result of that union. He must have spent the rest of his life in fear of being caught, for in those days he would have been either hanged from the ship's yard-arm or flogged round the Fleet.

My great-grandfather, Alexander Wilson, had been one of the most successful businessmen in the North of Scotland. A solid citizen and an elder of the 'Kirk', during the First World War, he had made a fortune from lucrative Government contracts, supplying the army with leather harnesses, saddles and traces from his large saddlery business. He was convinced that the horse was 'here to stay' and proclaimed that the new-fangled automobile was merely a passing fad. Needless to say, in this regard, he was not a man of farsightedness.

As a young boy I had to have lots of dental treatment. I loved sweets and chocolate and those together with the generally sweet Scottish diet played havoc with my teeth. Childhood at that time meant frequent trips to the dentist. In those days the 'School Dentist' perversely carried out fillings without any anaesthetics or painkillers and he became extremely annoyed if I showed any adverse reaction to this treatment. The pain was excruciating and I howled and struggled through years of his treatments, dragged along by my unsympathetic mother who had a great admiration and unswerving, blind faith in the medical profession: a faith which she still has to this day.

Chapter 2

An Illustrious Ancestor

by Malcolm

T he fact that I had to endure countless tortures in the dentist's chair with no relief for pain is somewhat ironic, as my great-great-uncle on my fathers' side of the family was Professor Sir James Young Simpson, who in 1847 discovered chloroform and became the father of modern anaesthetics. He was also a great man of God. Successive generations throughout the world owe a great debt of gratitude to this man's simple Christian faith and God-given ingenuity. In those days surgery was something that was regarded with considerable fear and dread, for there were no anaesthetics or painkillers. A good surgeon of the day was one who could saw off a leg in a minute or less. Most patients had to be held down by several strong men and strapped to a wooden operating table, often dying of shock even before the scalpel was applied, or from septicaemia afterwards. Childbirth too, was agony for most women at that time and the mother and infant mortality rate was very high. The young James Simpson, of Huguenot descent, born on 7th June 1811, and brought up as a Bible-believing Christian by his farmer father, was agonised by the heart-rending screams of his patients. Simpson was convinced that it was not God's will that people should suffer in this way and determined that he would find a potion or draught that would render his patients insensible and therefore impervious to pain.

He established a laboratory in his house in Edinburgh and

worked long into the early hours after his day's work. He and his assistants would try out various cocktails of chemicals and medicines on themselves, often with extremely unpleasant results. One night in November 1847, Simpson mixed together a potion comprising mainly of formyle of chloroform. He and his assistants inhaled the fumes deeply and promptly passed out. Several hours later they came to and realised that they had discovered the first effective anaesthetic. The effect of this remarkable discovery on medical practice of those days is hard to imagine now. Today we take so many things for granted. Brain and heart surgery, organ transplants and cosmetic surgery are relatively common place, but none of these procedures would be possible were it not for what happened that Saturday evening in Edinburgh, one hundred and fifty years ago. Professor Simpson's operations were transformed. He had conquered pain! The word spread like wildfire.

People everywhere clamoured to be his patients. (It is true that Lister had introduced ether from the USA where it had been used as an anaesthetic previously, but Simpson found it unreliable, too volatile and its effects on his patients unpredictable.)

The Duchess of Argyll expressed her feelings in a letter she wrote when chloroform was but a month old:

> 'Dear Dr Simpson, I cannot resist one line to wish you joy of your discovery. I think your life must be a very happy one from the relief of **not** witnessing pain, which it must be as painful to see as to bear. It must make you very happy, dear sir, to have discovered so great a boon. Next to the cure of souls, there can be no more wonderful blessing bestowed on man than to have been allowed the possession of such a "gift of healing." '

One might think that everyone would be of the same opinion and that people everywhere would be delighted with Simpson's new discovery. However he faced fierce and determined opposition from the establishment. The Church declared that his discovery undermined religion:

'To try to remove the primal curse on women was to fight against divine law; God had **meant** women to suffer during childbirth! ... Simpson's discovery was the very work of the Devil.'

He was condemned from every pulpit in the land. In his paper *The Defence of Anaesthesia*, he countered the scriptural objections and quoted from James 4:7:

' *"Therefore to him that knoweth to do good and doeth it not, to him it is sin,"* – if we followed the letter of the Word without the Spirit thereof, not only would the daughters of Eve have to obey the law and suffer, but the sons of Adam must adhere literally also to the decree of the curse and hence must earn their bread by the sweat of their face, and by that only. In regard to the primary curse the word translated "sorrow" is truly labour, toil and in the very next verse the very same word means this. Adam was to eat of the ground with "sorrow". This does not mean **physical** pain, and it was cursed to bear thorns and thistles, which we pull up without dreaming that it is a sin. Besides, Jesus Christ in dying surely hath borne our griefs and carried our sorrows and removed the curse of the law, being made a curse for us. We may rest fully and perfectly assured that whatever is true in point of fact, or humane, and merciful in point of practice will find no condemnation in the Word of God. Jesus' mission was to introduce mercy, not sacrifice.'

To an Irish lady who asked him, 'Is it not against nature to take away the pangs of labour?' Simpson replied, 'Is it not unnatural for you to have been carried over from Ireland in a steamboat against wind and tide?'

He encountered equal measures of ridicule and opposition from his peers in the medical profession. Learned men proclaimed that, 'the cold steel of the surgeons knife was an efficacious tonic,' and that 'no self-respecting physician should contemplate this new fangled dangerous procedure.' A leading medical contemporary objected to chloroform on the grounds that, 'It does nothing but "save pain." '

Simpson replied:

> 'A carriage does nothing but save fatigue. Which is most important to get done away with? Your fatigue, or your patient's screams and tortures?
>
> To confess to you the truth, my blood feels chilled by the inhumanity and deliberate cruelty which you and some members of your profession openly avow.
>
> And I know that you will yet, in a few years, look back with horror at your present resolution of refusing to relieve your patients, merely because you have not yet had time to get rid of some old professional caprices and nonsensical thoughts upon the subject.'

The American Civil War of the 1860s was a source of great excitement to him. He had patients and pupils in both North and South and many animated discussions arose among Americans from both sides who met in his drawing room, whilst visiting his busy house in Queen Street, Edinburgh. Dr George Otis, US Army reported:

> 'Ether is not suited for use on the battlefield, because it is impossible for the attendants to carry an adequate quantity upon the actual field; whereas a surgeon may take on his person, in a flask, a sufficient quantity of chloroform to produce anaesthesia in all the cases he is likely to be called upon to attend. In our unhappy struggle, chloroform was administered in more than one hundred and twenty thousand cases.'

Physician to rich and poor alike, this humble man, whose discovery of chloroform had been used in the delivery of many of Queen Victoria's children, came to be feted by most of the crowned heads of Europe. In 1866 he received the following letter:

> 'Osborne, 3rd January 1866
>
> Dear Dr Simpson,
> Your professional merits, especially your introduction of chloroform, by which difficult operations in surgery

have been rendered painless, and which has in many cases made that possible which would otherwise have been too hazardous to attempt, deserve some special recognition from the Crown.

The Queen has been pleased to command me to offer you on these grounds the rank of Baronet. I trust it will be agreeable to you to accept the offer.

I remain, yours very truly

Russell'

Within a few years of its discovery the apothecary, 'Duncan and Flockhart' of Edinburgh were producing nearly a million doses of this new wonder potion per week. Simpson made no financial gain from his discovery. He sought no patent rights or exclusive benefit. Chloroform was to be made available to all. One of his patients was the wife of the famous preacher Charles H. Spurgeon, who lay near death until saved by Simpson's timely intervention. He never took a fee from clergymen or their families. Instead Simpson would tell them:

'I'll wait till you are archbishops, meanwhile I'll take my fee in your prayers, as the prayer of a righteous man availeth much.'

Professor Simpson joined the Free Church movement in 1843. He rebelled at what he believed to be religious oppression; but at the same time, rigidly truthful, he refused to become an elder of the church, because of certain doctrines in the Confessions of faith with which he did not agree. When he died at the early age of fifty-nine, from overwork and the cumulative effects on his body of his self-administered experiments, his family were offered almost the equivalent of a state funeral, to be held in London, with a procession to Westminster Abbey where his coffin would be interred and where a grateful nation could pay their respects. In the event, the family decided that he should be buried in the city he loved. His funeral at Warriston Cemetery, attracted thousands of people who came to pay him homage from all over the world, including many members of the British and European Royal families. On his simple tombstone was carved the inscription, 'Nevertheless I live'.

The whole city of Edinburgh came to a standstill, and out of respect for the great man, every business in the city closed for the day. He was honoured by the nation in Westminster Abbey and a bronze bust of Simpson can still be seen there today. He played a leading part in the 1859 revival and although not a man of the cloth, felt it his duty to preach the Gospel of Jesus Christ publicly, during this period. This did not go down well with many members of the medical profession. His public confession of faith was looked upon as a piece of eccentric cant at which they shrugged their shoulders, and used as a handle to belittle him. But Sir James was not a man to allow this kind of treatment to deflect him from his faith.

Near the end of his distinguished life, when asked by an interviewer, 'Professor Simpson, What do you consider was the greatest discovery you ever made?' the great man simply replied, 'That I had a Saviour, in the Lord Jesus Christ.'

(All references and quotes are reproduced from *Sir James Young Simpson*, written by his daughter Eve Blantyre Simpson, and published by Oliphant, Anderson & Perrier in 1896. Bible references are from the Authorised King James Bible.)

Chapter 3

I Make my Way in Life
by Malcolm

M y best friend was Robert Johannesson whose father
was a lay preacher and held Gospel mission meetings
in a large tent. My recollection of these meetings is vague,
but I know I enjoyed them. Mr Johannesson senior was a
strictly no-nonsense preacher. Salvation was a serious
matter, but I remember him as a friendly man and he made
the most delicious Christmas pudding I have ever tasted.
Mrs Johannesson was friendly but firm, in the manner you
would expect in a strict religious home. Although I attended
their mission meetings on several occasions and heard the
Gospel preached many times, the message of salvation
through Jesus Christ, at that time was lost on me, although
I can see now that a seed was planted then that would not
grow until many years later.

Adolescence

In 1962 my father was promoted to a new job within the
British Egg Marketing Board and one day announced we
were moving to Taunton in Somerset down in England. So
several weeks later, one chilly August day in Aberdeen, my
mother, baby sister and I boarded the overnight sleeper train
at the station and began our journey southwards. My
brother John had by this time completed his national service
in the army and was managing a tea plantation in Assam,
Northern India.

We arrived in the sleepy little market town of Taunton late next afternoon and I remember it was very hot. I had not experienced such weather before; it was completely different from the climate I had grown up in. One month later when the local schools returned from holiday, at the age of fifteen, I began a two-year 'O' level course at Priorswood Co-Educational school, now re-named St. Augustines (see Postscript on page 145). For the first time since I was eleven, I found myself sitting next to girls. They teased me mercilessly about my Scottish accent and I soon lost it!

I became amazed at the difference between the Scottish and English Educational systems. The English system was much more democratic. Pupils were allowed to have opinions and encouraged to discuss the merits of differing philosophies, traditions, and beliefs, albeit within the guidelines of the curriculum. Self-expression and original thought were actively encouraged. But I had too long been a prisoner of my upbringing and the Scottish system to instantly adjust to my new found freedom. It was several years before I became confident enough to express myself freely and finally break loose from the shackles which had been forged in my early years.

The early Sixties were remarkable for the many social and political changes that took place worldwide, particularly in Britain at that time, the so-called Cultural Revolution. There was a general feeling of confidence in the country. British pop music, led by the Beatles and the Stones and British fashion led by Mary Quant and featuring the mini-skirt, was taking the world by storm. British theatre was breaking new ground with plays such as *Look back in Anger*, by John Osborne. Movies such as, *The L-Shaped Room*, *Saturday Night and Sunday Morning* and *The Loneliness of the Long Distance Runner*, were changing the face of the British film industry. Television too was experiencing this 'new age', and 'kitchen sink' drama became the 'in' thing. BBC TV's *Play for Today* became more and more daring. Realism was in! After years of post-war drabness, Britain was the centre of world attention.

'Out with the old in with the new!' was the mood of the day. Even the Church was trying to appeal to the youth of the day. Guitars and amplifiers began to appear in some churches and many clergymen were anxious to be seen to be 'cool'. Sex, previously a taboo subject, generally confined to marriage, became the main preoccupation of most teenagers and young people, including myself. The Pill 'liberated' women and in a pre-AIDS climate, sexual promiscuity became the norm. James Bond, was the definitive role model for most red-blooded males. Women were disposable sex-objects to be used casually, then discarded for another. The early Sixties was the turning point which I believe marked the beginning of the rapid descent into the morass the world finds itself in now.

I passed my 'O' level exams and I could have gone on to Grammar school to study for 'A' levels but I decided that I'd had enough of studying and at the age of seventeen I joined a large chain of newsagents as a Management trainee, where I thought I might learn about retailing and make my way in life. I was surrounded by women of all ages and was quite shy at first, but soon came out of my shell.

Leaving Home

In 1966 I was transferred to work in the West End of London. It was a tremendous adventure. London in the swinging sixties! I rented a room in a shared house in Cricklewood, North London and spent the next five years learning to drive, learning to drink, learning how to charm women, and learning to live a generally aimless existence. I passed my driving test at the age of twenty and bought my first car.

In December 1969 I met my first wife Angela. A passionate love affair led us to live together almost immediately. Angela was five years older than I and was a mature, attractive woman. She was loving, patient, kind and was 'all for me'. I in return was jealous, moody, irritable, subject to outbursts of bad temper and wanted everything my own way. I was difficult to live with, insecure and all in all a real hypocrite, but only in private. I kept my true nature well hidden from everyone but Angela. I was out of work at that time for a few months but eventually obtained a job as salesman for the Southern bottler of Coca-Cola. It was hard work, but I learned fast and as I applied myself, my career as a salesman began to prosper. We were married in 1972 and I was given a transfer to Coca-Cola's operation in the West of England and we bought a small house in a place called Yate, a small dormitory town near my parent's house in Downend, Bristol. For a while I was contented, but I was very ambitious and with two middle-aged managers above me, I could see little chance of promotion. So I applied for other jobs and in June 1973, I moved to a different company, Smiths Crisps Ltd (General Mills), in my first Sales Management position, as Sales Manager of a Mobile Sales team. In one move I doubled my salary, was given a generous expense allowance, a shiny new fast car and travelled around the country staying in smart hotels from Monday to Friday. It went straight to my head. I became very big-headed. I had a string of affairs with young women I met, mainly in clubs and bars. I was young, I had become confident, self-assured and I had lots of money. I was unfaithful, immoral and thought nothing of it.

Then the inevitable happened. I met someone and fell in love. I became totally besotted with an attractive nineteen-year old girl I met at the office. After a two-year affair, wrapped in a web of the usual lies and deceit, I left my wife Angela and set up home in the Midlands with Beth. I had changed jobs again by then and began a sales management job in Birmingham. Our relationship was passionate and stormy. I was worse than before, my character was just as bad as ever, but this time I was stricken with guilt over my treatment of Angela and I took this out on Beth at every opportunity. I seemed powerless to control my outbursts of jealous anger and I would actually begin to look for, or manipulate situations where I could attack Beth verbally, with no self-control or mercy. However whilst I insisted that she was faithful to me, I continued to be sexually promiscuous having numerous clandestine affairs with other women. I was a complete hypocrite and liar. At work I was unforgiving of other people's mistakes and developed a ruthlessness in business which brought excellent results in terms of sales and profitability, but made me no friends and brought me little happiness. I was a very unpleasant character who would step on anyone to get to the top.

Somehow Beth continued to put up with me and in 1980 several months after moving back to Coca-Cola as a Regional Sales Manager, we were married. Beth soon became pregnant with our first beautiful daughter, Adrienne. My career continued to flourish and by the time our lovely second daughter Winona was born in 1983, I was head of Sales and Distribution for Coca-Cola Beecham Bottlers, England and Wales, with more than 400 staff reporting to me through numerous line managers. Incredibly, my success at Coca-Cola was as a result of having a dream in 1982. At that time sales were bad, the company was going through a very rough patch and the pressure was on to reach very difficult sales targets. One night I dreamt of a completely new method of selling the company's products. This method utilised our existing resources, didn't increase costs at all, but greatly increased sales and market penetration. I even dreamed of the name for the operation – 'TRAC'. I presented it to my Sales Director and he immediately saw its potential and its importance to the company.

That summer I recruited a new Area Manager, Steve Hannington to manage the Midlands/South Wales area and soon discovered that we worked extremely well together. I remember one time he told me that his brother was a missionary.

'A missionary?' I scorned, conjuring up a picture of a large cooking pot surrounded by natives with some poor guy inside clutching his Bible!

'He must be mad.' I laughed.

Steve thought that it wasn't exactly his scene either.

Business continued to boom. I was given a free hand to introduce 'TRAC' to the whole company. In the first six months of operation, the company's sales increased dramatically and profits were up by over one million dollars! My 'TRAC' sales and marketing innovation contributed to the company becoming the most profitable soft drinks business in Europe. 'TRAC', which automatically became the property of my employers was later introduced with similar success into the Dutch and Scandinavian markets. I thought that I should be given a raise and further promotion and after a rather acrimonious session with a company director, who had claimed 'TRAC' as his own, I left Coca-Cola for a bigger job elsewhere. (At this time I lost touch with my friend Steve and was not to see him again for several years, by which time God had moved in his life and he was born again.)

In the spring of 1984 I joined another well-known drinks company and for the first few months everything went very well. I pleased my boss and I was relatively faithful to my wife as I had only one affair going on at the time. We had lots of material trappings of success, money, cars, foreign holidays etc. Life was good!

Then in July of that year something unusual happened, the sinister significance of which took some time to manifest.

Chapter 4

The Beginning of Sorrows

by Malcolm

During July 1984, I was leading a party of British salesmen on a visit to a supplier in Europe. Our host was a very wealthy and charming business man. At the end of one particular day, my colleagues were enjoying themselves in the hotel swimming pool and the host and myself were alone, having a drink at the hotel bar. He was well educated, married with a beautiful wife and children and spoke fluent English. He had been talking about his travels in South America, including some experiences of the occult (a word at that time which meant nothing to me) when suddenly, completely out of the blue, he said, 'Malcolm you look a bit tired, why don't we go and lie down in your room?'

'Pardon?' I spluttered. 'You heard me.' He replied.

I was dumbstruck. No man had ever made any such suggestion to me before. I had certainly done nothing to encourage him. I was just being friendly. Unfortunately I didn't handle the situation very well. I was highly embarrassed and muttered something about not being into that sort of thing. I hurriedly finished my drink and left the bar. He later cancelled the dinner appointment we had with him that night, was decidedly icy for the remaining two days of the trip, and did not speak to me again.

From that time on, everything changed and darkness entered my life.

When I got back to the UK my boss was suddenly moved sideways and my job performance which had been perfectly acceptable only weeks before, was no longer good enough for my new master. After a few more difficult months, despite achieving the best sales increase in the company, I was sacked with a six-month salary pay off. By this time I was completely disillusioned with working for large companies and I decided to start my own business. My wife was in agreement and after spending six months planning and researching the market, we took out a bigger mortgage on our house, and in May 1985, opened a kitchenware shop in a shopping mall in the town where we lived. For the next seven months, business went exactly to plan.

Lloyds Bank were amazed. When you want to borrow from a bank to start a business, you have to provide them with a detailed business plan forecasting on a weekly basis sales, costs, profit etc. For the first seven months of trading actual sales figures were within an incredible £75.00 of those I had forecast! Sales were rising, profits growing – the outlook was rosy. I thought life was wonderful and at last we were going to be OK. I had settled down to family life and had no girlfriends at the time. I was relatively happy.

Then a tragic event took place in January 1986, which was to trigger off a series of seemingly unrelated events, which were the beginning of great sorrows in my life and which brought me to the edge of the abyss. A young woman was savagely murdered in the multi-storey car park adjacent to our shop. It took the police six months to detect and arrest the murderer. During that time the car park remained virtually deserted and as 95% of our customers were women who normally used this particular car park, our sales takings plummeted from £3,000.00 per week on average, to less than £200.00 per week. We weren't even covering our costs!

Eventually the police arrested and charged a young student with the murder. He lived two houses along the road from where we lived! My wife Beth had always felt that there was something creepy about him. I started up yet another business in order to get out of trouble but this endeavour eventually failed too. Somehow I had to continue to service our large bank loan and mortgage, so I got non-salaried, commission only jobs, selling kitchens and replacement windows. They brought in some money, but not enough. I was at my wit's end! Things couldn't possibly get worse, I thought. But I was wrong – they did!

To cap it all, a main drain backed up outside. We had a flood of sewage through the kitchenware shop, the entire inventory was ruined and I had to close the business down. At that time we were deeply in debt and owed money to the bank, the building society, and my father-in-law. I wanted to sell our large house and move to a smaller one and discharge our debts, but my wife wouldn't hear of it. Our marriage began to suffer quite badly. One early morning in June 1987, after many sleepless nights, I found myself stumbling through the town at six o'clock in the morning, trying desperately to figure a way out of our difficulties. I found myself trying the doors of several local churches, but they were all locked and barred. I don't really know what I expected to find there. I guess I was seeking help from the Lord even then, although I didn't know Him. Nevertheless, in my helplessness and frustration, I shook my fist to the heavens and blamed all my misfortune on Him!

There was a deafening silence. If there was a God, He wasn't taking any notice of somebody like me!

Somehow though we managed to survive. I started a business which was quite profitable producing CVs/Resumes on a word processor which my wife ran from home. I managed to get someone interested in taking on the lease of what was now our empty shop and at last I was successful in obtaining an excellent Sales and Marketing position with a manufacturing company in the South of England. The salary was very good, the most I had ever earned, and although it meant I had to be away from home, Monday to Friday, I had no alternative but to take it.

We gradually began to get out of debt and within a few months we had a nanny, a housekeeper and a secretary to help my wife with the expanding CV/Resume business. We began to live well again. I quickly forgot about my search for the Lord. But quite suddenly during 1988, my wife seemed to dramatically change. Her heart became hard towards me and unfortunately our marriage began to disintegrate rapidly. Suddenly I realised that I did not want to lose my wife and children, but Beth had had enough. She wanted a life without me. Somehow I persuaded her that we should try marriage counselling and for a while we were reconciled. She became pregnant again in Summer 1988. When it was confirmed, I was delighted, I had always wanted a son and after two daughters, maybe this one would be a boy. But she was horrified at the prospect and insisted on having an abortion. I tried desperately to dissuade her, but it was no use. There was nothing I could do. In this country a father has no rights concerning his unborn child. I was completely heartbroken and shattered, but I had no choice in the matter and I reluctantly agreed to pay for the operation.

A new secretary came to work for me the day before my wife was due to have the operation. She saw my distressed condition and enquired what was wrong. I said it was a private matter. (I had discussed the matter with no-one and was not about to do so.) She smiled and gave me a piece of paper with a phone number on it. She told me her father had recently gone through a difficult time and a local woman had been of great help, and she read tarot cards. I said that I had read horoscopes in the papers, now and then, but I didn't really believe in all that stuff. But for some reason, I kept the phone number anyway.

That night I was gripped by incredible sadness and pain and on impulse I phoned the number from my hotel room and made an appointment to see Helen at 8.00 pm. I duly arrived at the address she had given me and said to the attractive young woman who opened the door that I didn't really know why I had come, that I didn't really believe in all this and that was all I was going to say. I didn't want to give her any clues about me. I really was in two minds about stepping into her house at all, but I threw caution to the wind and went inside. Helen said that I didn't have to say anything at all and that she would simply read the cards for me. She led me into a perfectly ordinary sitting room, opened a drawer, pulled out a bundle wrapped in a red velvet cloth and unwrapped a pack of what looked like very large playing cards. She asked me to shuffle the cards which I did and handed them back to her. She then asked me to pick out twelve cards at random and place them face down on the floor. Neither she nor I could see what the cards were, until she turned the first card over. A look of anguish appeared on her face,

'Why is your wife doing this to your baby?' asked Helen softly.

I promptly burst into tears.

When I had recovered she then explained the meaning of the rest of the cards with equal accuracy. She told me about my past life, relationships with women, my previous marriage, my devious nature, my present job and the immediate future. I was hooked. I consulted Helen at least every month for the next year. In the meantime nearly all of her predictions came about.

Beth and I finally parted in November 1988 with much acrimony and bitterness on both sides. I suspected that there was another man on the scene and this was soon confirmed. I found this parting almost impossible to bear. I felt cheated, betrayed and angry. Although I had been unfaithful as well, I would never have left Beth and my children. All my worst suspicions and fears about women had been confirmed. The rug had been pulled from underneath my feet – I had lost everything, wife, family and home. Life was unbearable.

(At this time I had no knowledge of the biblical principle of sowing and reaping.)

One night in my lonely hotel room I felt utterly and desperately unhappy. I felt actual physical, leaden pain in the pit of my stomach. I was angry, jealous and helpless. I began to flick through the pages of the Gideon's Bible which was on the table. As I read the words nothing really registered, but a faint echo of something, I don't know what, made me turn to read the prayer Jesus taught His disciples:

> 'Our Father, who art in Heaven,
> Hallowed be Thy name,
> Thy Kingdom come,
> Thy will be done,
> On earth as it is in Heaven,
> Give us today our daily bread,
> Forgive us our debts
> As we forgive our debtors,

> *Lead us not into temptation*
> *But deliver us from the evil one*
> *For thine is the Kingdom*
> *The Power and the Glory*
> *For ever and ever*
> *Amen.'*

I then felt I had to read it out loud, so every night from then on, I read the Lord's prayer out loud before I went to sleep. (I have also taught my children to do the same ever since.)

Nothing happened. If God really existed where was He? I was so miserable at this time, and at such a loss as to what to do next, that Helen suggested I go and see her friend, Bill, who she described as a faith healer and medium. In December 1988, I met Bill, a sprightly old gentleman in his late sixties. He answered the door with a smile and bade me come in, remarking that he thought we had met before. I said that I thought not. He introduced me to his friend Theresa, a very pleasant woman in her fifties and then showed me into a dining room where the two of us could be alone and handed me a notepad and a pencil. He sat opposite me across the dining table which was covered in a brown velvet tablecloth.

He began to run a finger over a few square inches of tablecloth in front of him, tracing little patterns as if doodling. Then he began to smile and tell me about my life in great detail with knowledge of me that Helen did not have and about intimate things that I had told absolutely no-one. Bill still had the curious little smile on his face as he told me that I was looking for a small house to rent because I was fed up having lived in a hotel room for the better part of a whole year. He described several houses which I would be looking at and finally a small cottage which I would finally decide upon. He even described the wallpaper in the sitting room and the type of winter flowering shrub growing on the trellis on the porch, outside the front door. He told me that I would not be there long though, then described another building of Victorian red brick and dark oak panelling where I would move to in a few months time.

The building, he said, was the only one of its type in the area and he thought somewhere in Scotland. I was amazed at the detail and wrote it all down in the notepad he had provided. I gave him £10.00 which seemed to be the going rate, and joined him and Theresa for tea and biscuits. They were very ordinary, friendly, gentle folk who seemed to have a genuine heart for people. That night I prayed my prayer as usual and said, 'I don't know if I'm doing the right thing here, but if there really is a God and you can hear me, please help me. If this is wrong, please keep me on the right path.'

Two days later I moved out of my hotel and into a small cottage in the village of Shillington, which was exactly as Bill described it, right down to the wallpaper in the sitting room and the winter flowering bush on the porch trellis by the front door.

Three weeks after that, I was called into my Managing Director's office and was told that my division was relocating to Hawick in Scotland and that I could either relocate there or become redundant. This news came as a complete surprise, something of a shock in fact, despite Bill's prediction. The company had just bought another similar operation to mine, which no-one had been told about including me until then, because the move involved a merger and inevitable job losses.

One month later, on 14th February 1989 I checked into the Kirklands Hotel in the little town of Hawick in the Scottish Borders. The hotel was a rather imposing grey building, with a light and airy interior, not at all as Bill had described. I signed the register, collected my key and was directed to the nearby annexe. As I walked through the pleasant gardens full of thick bushes and shrubs, I turned a corner and there in front of me, was the annexe – a large red stone Victorian building with dark oak panelled interiors. This building I soon discovered was unique and had been built of red sandstone by the original rich owners who had the stones brought up from England as there was no red stone in this part of Scotland. Bill had also foretold that I would work in an office building in the centre of Hawick which was pointed like the bow of a ship, at the junction of two streets and which had a fabulous view of the local hills with 'a boy on a horse' outside in the street. After checking into my room, I found my way to the company's factory premises on the outskirts of Hawick and it didn't look anything like this description.

At the end of the week, I had to find a small office from which to run my CV business and engage a secretary to handle the correspondence, while I continued to manage the window company. That Friday morning after a few days looking around, I signed a short-term lease on the only suitable small office available in the town. I noticed as I signed the document that the owner's large office was a curious shape, coming to a point like the bow of a ship where the two streets met outside and that immediately outside his window in the street below, was a life-size bronze statue of a boy astride a large horse.

Bill had said I would learn to speak a **new language** before the end of the year, which would be very important to me and open many doors! I thought that he must be mad, the only language I could speak was English and I had no inclination to learn another. He went on to tell me that he saw me in a small boat on a very stormy sea, with no oars and no sails. Then he saw a large hand throwing me a rope which I gratefully grabbed, whereupon I was pulled to the shore and safety! He also described my being handed a clean sheet of paper and that someone was going to give me a 'fresh start'! I asked him what this new language was and he said although he could hear me speaking it he couldn't understand it and that it sounded strange, possibly German. I didn't understand any of this and he said he didn't either. He went on to tell me he could see me speaking this language in a large 'green' auditorium with a stage. There was the sound of 'beautiful singing'. It was a very 'spiritual' place, he said. I was completely mystified and baffled as to what it all could mean.

I was unhappy in Hawick and had been applying for jobs back in England. I handed Bill an envelope I had received regarding a forthcoming job interview and by merely holding it and without opening it, he was able to tell me the type of company (Soft Drinks) and even details about the secretary who had typed the letter! He said the colour 'orange' came to mind and that the Managing Director was a black man who came from a very hot island and that his secretary spoke fluent German and was a very good skier. He also said the location of the company was near the 'sound of money'. Two weeks later I attended the interview at the orange juice plant, near the Royal Mint in South Wales where pound coins were manufactured. The MD was a native West Indian and his secretary Monica was Czechoslovakian. She had been born on the German border, spoke fluent German and had learned to ski when she was three years old! (I was later offered the job!)

Bill became very strange during this last session when I began to question him about a number of things.

A strange thing had occurred one night in the Farmhouse Hotel in Hertfordshire where I had been staying for several months. A few days before I met Helen and later Bill, early one morning about 4 am, I suddenly awoke and realised there was someone standing right next to my bed. The room was in complete darkness and I opened my eyes and saw a figure about six feet tall. I could not make out any discernible features, as this figure seemed to consist entirely of brilliant light. The odd thing was that the light was contained within the figure and did not illuminate the room. I was startled and shouted out, at the same time reaching for the light switch. When the light went on the figure instantly disappeared. I felt that this person had been there for some time. I felt peace and love had been in that room.

I also somehow felt that this figure had been watching over me and understood my sadness and pain, I felt reassured and fell asleep again. (In Hebrews 1:14 the scripture says of the angels, *'Are they not all ministering spirits sent forth to minister for those who will inherit salvation?'*)

I asked Bill about this figure and about Jesus and he ground to a complete halt, somehow frozen in motion. After about half a minute I realised Bill was no longer there and that I was now talking directly to someone other than Bill. As I looked, Bill's facial muscles actually began to re-arrange themselves so much so, that his countenance became completely changed. This other person described himself as 'an ascendent Master' and claimed that he had been a doctor in South Africa during the Boer War. He told me that I too, had many lives before and that I was being 'perfected' in this one. For some reason I asked him if Jesus was there, where he was, and he said, 'Oh, you mean the Nazarene – yes he's here somewhere.'

He told me quite sternly not to put Bill under pressure with any more questions and that he would return presently. After a minute or so Bill 'returned', his face gradually became normal and he had no recollection of this discussion. It was at this time I began to become very suspicious and felt that I was being led up the 'garden path' by these entities whoever they were.

A month or so later, during May 1989, I had to travel to Southampton in the South of England on business and I phoned my old friend Steve Hannington and arranged to visit him and his new wife. Steve offered me dinner and a bed for the night, so I gratefully accepted. I arrived a little early in a town in Hampshire called Fleet, which I had never visited before, so I took the time to buy a bottle of rather good wine, then made my way to Steve's house. After an early dinner Steve, Katy his wife, and I sat and talked about our spiritual experiences. Steve told me how he had come to Fleet after he had separated from his ex-wife, had found Jesus and become born again. I didn't really understand what he was talking about, but decided to humour him anyway. He seemed to have changed, he no longer swore or told risque jokes. All in all he seemed very boring to me.

I shared with my hosts the last few years of my life, how my second marriage had failed and how I had discovered comfort in my new found 'spiritual' friends, Helen and Bill. Steve immediately became concerned, told me that it was all wrong and showed me passages from the Bible concerning divination and mediums. I politely agreed to disagree. He read me a few more passages concerning Jesus, which I recognised as part of the Gospel message. Next morning I carried on my journey and promised to keep in touch. I thought that although Steve was no longer the person I used to know, he seemed happier and more at peace with himself.

If this was a result of his new found 'religion', then that was OK for him, but definitely not for me!

(Steve told me some months later after I was saved, that he was not looking forward to my visit and that he had asked the whole of his house-group round to pray in every room of his house before I arrived!)

Near the end of July, I phoned Helen, and discovered that she had been quite ill. I asked her if she would like to travel up to Hawick to recuperate and she replied that she would love to. We had become good friends and I looked forward to seeing her again. She had little money of her own, so I paid for the single air ticket by credit card and arranged to drive her home again. I had to return south before the end of the month to start my new job in South Wales as the CEO (Chief Executive Officer) of the orange juice company, having been made redundant when the manufacturing company in Hawick finally went bust.

She arrived that night near the end of July 1989. It was raining heavily when I met her at Edinburgh airport and she looked very pale. She was pleased to see me and I her. We drove the fifty plus miles or so back to my spacious three-bedroomed company apartment in Hawick, which I retained the use of, as part of my redundancy package with my ex-employers. I cooked her some pasta, opened a bottle of Chianti and after dinner we sat and chatted. She suffered from a bone disease, a sort of osteoporosis and was having to take frequent painkillers, as the pain became unbearable. She explained that she was recovering from one of these attacks. I had prepared a spare room for her, but she had other ideas and we ended up in my room. I was lonely, she was attractive, available and the inevitable happened.

Chapter 5

The Mask Drops

by Malcolm

N ext day as the weather was hot and sunny, we decided to tour around the locality. Helen wanted to visit the Sami Ling Tibetan Buddhist Temple in Eskerdale Valley near Hawick, which she had read about although I myself had never heard of it. As we rounded the bend in the road, the sight which greeted us was astonishing. I couldn't believe my eyes. Here in the middle of the Scottish Borders, of all places, was a large golden pagoda, with peacocks, flowing streams etc. It looked just like something straight out of the Orient. Helen talked privately to the head man, a Tibetan monk, for about half an hour. We wandered around the place for a while and then returned to Hawick. Later that evening, Helen began to act strangely. One time she would become suddenly very sarcastic about me, another time, extremely abusive. I gradually began to discern at least four distinctive and separate personalities which had not revealed themselves previously, and they were all quite nasty. I began to be troubled. When she was in control of herself again she could remember nothing about these others and began to become concerned when I told her. She said she did not want to become a trance medium.

The following day we met a couple of people who lived and worked near Hawick. They had a kiln and made strange little figures and various pots and statues. They gave us tea and explained they believed in wood spirits, fairies and the like. The woman practised spiritual healing and reflexology.

They talked about the power of colours, and suchlike. They suggested that Helen should visit their friend who was a faith-healer in Dumfries and also suggested that Iona was a very special place and well worth a visit. (Iona is a small island off the West Coast of Scotland, where St. Columba first stepped ashore in 563 AD, bringing Christianity to Scotland.) Next day Helen became very ill and was in considerable pain. Her painkillers weren't working and I became extremely worried about her. She wanted to go and see the man in Dumfries so I agreed to take her there right away. She phoned him up, made the arrangements and off we went. We arrived about 2 pm, by which time Helen was in a dreadful state. She was racked with pain, crying pitifully and could hardly walk. I practically carried her into the examination room and Mr Carlton and myself lifted her onto the treatment couch. He asked her a few questions and opened a glass display cabinet containing what looked like lots of coloured glass rods. These were the crystals he said he used to heal people. He selected a few, placing them under her back, on her forehead and at other points which he called 'Chakras'.

He then held a long green glass rod and passed it along the length of her body, about a foot above it, whilst laying the other hand on various areas of her anatomy. She was fully clothed and everything was done in a proper manner. After about twenty minutes of this, the effect was dramatic. Helen had completely recovered, the pain had gone and she was sitting up laughing and chatting. We thanked Mr Carlton paid him his fee of £30.00 and chatted to him over a cup of tea. I asked him lots of questions, mentioned Jesus and asked him what he thought. He replied, 'Oh, the Nazarene again,' and was quite dismissive about Him. I couldn't think why I kept asking these people about Jesus. We continued on our way to Iona which we reached next day. Helen said it was a place of great spiritual significance. I thought it was unusual with such white sand and clear blue water, but felt nothing else about it. We wandered about and bought some souvenirs from the Abbey, like regular tourists. The island attracts people of every type of spiritual belief and religion; from Buddhists to spiritualists, you can find them all on Iona, rather like Glastonbury in Somerset, England.

During Helen's second week with me, in the last week of July 1989, when we were back in Hawick, we were lying in bed about to fall asleep, I suddenly became aware of presences in the room. I quickly switched on the light but could see nothing. Helen had felt them too but was unperturbed. I got back in bed and felt peculiar sensations in my stomach, high up, just under my rib cage accompanied by loud rumbling noises. Suddenly I felt I was being held down. I felt strange painful sensations in the back of my head and in my arms and legs, and suddenly I felt as if I were floating up, leaving my body. These continued for a few minutes and then stopped. I felt as if my body had been somehow invaded. It was the most terrifying experience of my life.

Next day we were in Edinburgh, sitting on a park bench in the famous Princess Street Gardens waiting for the one o'clock gun to fire, when Helen began to speak in a strange voice. Suddenly, there was an unpleasant peculiar smell about her, which I could only describe as something like rotten eggs. The voice claimed to be that of an aunt of mine who had died a few years previously. She said that I had to be good and not resist them, because they were only trying to do me good.

'**No way**,' I thought.

By this time I'd had enough. Something inside me sensed that this was all wrong, I began reciting the Lord's prayer in my mind and the voice emanating from Helen stopped immediately and then demanded 'that I should stop that at once.' I said that I'd had enough of this. I grabbed Helen by the hand and we walked quickly to the car. I bundled her in and drove up and down looking for a church – any church! I parked outside a large old-fashioned church in the middle of Edinburgh. Helen refused to go inside – but I dragged her in. The place was empty so we sat at the front and I recited once more the Lord's prayer – only this time out loud! Immediately a tremendous sense of peace and safety enveloped us. Helen said later that she had never felt anything like it. After about half an hour we left the church and immediately as we came out, a car sped towards us the wrong way down the one way street, and drove into the side of my car. I felt that something or someone had tried to injure or kill us.

The driver was a young man and was practically incoherent, although there was no alcohol on his breath. He said he was very sorry, and seemed dazed and confused not knowing where he was or what he was doing. The damage was not serious so we went back to Hawick. Helen was deeply affected by the experience in the church and swore never to touch tarot cards or the like ever again. As we drove along she fell asleep and after about half an hour, still fast asleep she said in a soft voice, 'Malcolm, be faithful and true.' I didn't know what she meant and when I asked her later, she could not remember saying anything at all.

That night, we went to a friend's house for dinner out in the country where we met again the people who had the kiln. Helen rode our host's pony for a while as we waited to eat. Just before the meal was ready Helen asked me to get her some cigarettes from a nearby pub. As I was coming back down the dark country lane on foot, I was suddenly gripped with indescribable terror. A dreadful fear flowed down through my body from the top of my head to the soles of my feet. It was a very physical sensation. It overwhelmed me and shook me to the core.

I have never experienced anything like it before or since. I was still shaking when I got back to the cottage. The meal was strange, a kind of beef stew, with whole large mushrooms. It smelt awful and tasted odd and I could only eat about half of it. After about fifteen minutes I had to go to the bathroom. I had acute and extremely violent, painful diahorrea, I felt my body was rejecting whatever it was I had eaten. Somehow I managed to get through the rest of the evening, but I felt dizzy, very strange and somehow drugged.

In the meantime, Helen had changed personality again and said that she had decided that there was nothing wrong with her tarot readings, that she had been given a gift and that she would continue to use it, 'to help people'. If I had any sense at all I should have packed her off home on a plane, right there and then, but it was past midnight so I determined to part company with her next day at the very first opportunity. We were lying in bed back in the flat in

Hawick when in the early hours of Thursday morning, I felt again those unseen presences trying to invade my body. The pain was intense. I felt drugged and unable to resist. Helen told me to relax and not fight them. I wasn't having any of it. This was all wrong. Somehow I managed to grab my Gideon's Bible which I had taken with me from the hotel in England. (Gideon's, I owe you one Bible.) I struggled to my feet, stark naked, switched on the light and opened the Bible, flicking through its pages, desperately looking for I knew not what. My eyes fell on these passages from Revelation chapter 19, which I began to shout out, in a loud voice!

> 'And I heard, as it were, the voice of a great multitude, as the sound of many waters and as the sound of mighty thunderings, saying, "Alleluia! For the Lord God Omnipotent reigns! Let us be glad and rejoice and give Him the glory, for the marriage of the Lamb has come, and His wife has made herself ready." And to her it was granted to be arrayed in fine linen, clean and bright, for the fine linen is the righteous acts of the saints. Then he said to me, "Write: 'Blessed are those who are called to the marriage supper of the Lamb!'" And he said to me, "These things are the true sayings of God." And I fell at his feet to worship him. But he said to me, "See that you do not do that! I am your fellow servant, and of your brethren who have the testimony of Jesus. Worship God! For the testimony of Jesus is the spirit of prophecy." Then I saw heaven opened, and behold, a white horse. And He who sat on him was called Faithful and True, and in righteousness He judges and makes war. His eyes were like a flame of fire, and on His Head were many crowns. He had a name written that no one knew except Himself. He was clothed with a robe dipped in blood, and His name is called The Word of God. And the armies in heaven, clothed in fine linen, white and clean, followed Him on white horses. Now out of His mouth goes a sharp sword, that with it He should strike the nations. And He Himself will rule them with a rod of iron. He Himself treads the winepress of the fierceness and wrath of Almighty God. And He has on His robe and on His thigh a name written:
>
> KING OF KINGS AND LORD OF LORDS.'

Then something wonderful and incredible happened! In the next instant, in a twinkling of an eye, in a split second, **I knew exactly** who Jesus was!

Like looking through the lens of a camera, everything suddenly came into sharp focus.

(I discovered later that the Spirit moved on the Word and in that moment in time – ordained before the world was made – I was **convicted** of sin and righteousness and judgement. But I wasn't yet **saved**!) I had sunk into the very depths of sin and rebellion against God. But here He was – right there **with** me in the most terrible moment of my life. I shouted at those unseen forces to be gone – and they went!

'He **is** Faithful and True!' I cried out.

I then quickly got dressed and got out of that flat just as fast as I could. I knew that I had to get away. I jumped in my car and drove for miles and miles. My head was throbbing, I felt sick and ill. I could hardly see where I was going and was driving erratically. I was stopped and breathalysed by the Carlisle Motorway Police. The test was negative. They told me to drive to the nearby service area and get some coffee. On that Thursday morning at 7.30 am, I got a priest out of bed in Carlisle and asked him to pray for me in his church. I tried to tell him what had happened to me but he didn't really seem to understand. I was really afraid, shaking all over and still ill. The right side of my face felt somehow frozen or paralysed.

The day, **Thursday** was to have special significance some six months later. The priest prayed a simple prayer. He could see that something terrible had befallen me but he didn't seem to know what or how. I thanked him and left. The rest of the day I debated whether to go back to the flat or not. I didn't want to, but I had to get Helen back to Hertfordshire and out of my life! I returned to the flat about 4 pm. Helen was in a terrible state saying that she'd been worried sick about me. I bundled her things together and we were soon driving southwards. (I had to meet my parents next day to go to my uncle's funeral.)

About half-way there I suddenly felt dead tired. We had to get a motel room so I could get some sleep. Helen appeared to be listening to some unseen presence, some unheard voice.

'You must drink something,' she said and poured me a glass of water.

Immediately my stomach started rumbling again and I felt 'they' were back! I had no resistance but kept silently repeating the Lord's prayer over and over. I fell asleep and woke up a few hours later feeling terrible. We got back to Hertfordshire late that night and I slept in her bed with no more visitations. About 7 am, I got up and bade Helen a hasty goodbye, promising to call.

Friday passed quickly; my parents, my brother and I went to my uncle's funeral and then drove back to Bristol. I said nothing about my experiences; I was still in a state of shock. I was just thinking about going to bed when my mother suggested I might like a drink of orange juice. I declined, but she kept insisting. My father began to insist too. I began to think – they've been got at. That was it. I was out of the house pronto. I jumped in my car and drove around until I came to a Holiday Inn where I stayed the night. Early next day I went to a church near my parent's house. I went in, it was empty. I saw a niche in the wall near the door with some water in it. I drank some and splashed some on my head.

'Help me God!' I cried in desperation.

On returning to my parents house at mid-morning on Saturday, I made some excuse about having stayed out the night, collected my case, bade my folks a hurried farewell and left the house. What could I do? Where was I to go? I was even terrified of my own shadow. I felt I was being constantly watched by some unseen, evil presence that knew my every move.

I found myself driving to Fleet where my born again Christian friend, Steve Hannington lived. When I arrived, Steve and Katy were out. I didn't know anyone else in the town, so I drove about forty miles to see my friend of twelve years and best man at my second wedding, Andrew. He was pleased but surprised to see me. We went to his local wine bar and drank rather a lot of strong Belgian lager. Later we went to an expensive Indian restaurant and I bought the meal and two bottles of Bollinger Champagne. I tried to explain what had happened to me.

I told him I thought that beings from another world were right here on earth. That they had no bodies, were invisible and that their technology was thousands of years ahead of mankind's. I said that they were somehow connected with spiritualism and tarot cards in which he also was interested and that they were inherently evil. I said that I had decided I was going to be like one of Napoleon's Old Guard, at the Battle of Waterloo who gave the V sign to the Duke of Wellington's cannon rather than surrender.

'Eat drink and be merry,' I said, 'for tomorrow we die!' Andrew didn't think I was mad, or rather he didn't say so. He thought I had stumbled onto something. He suggested I try and find that place in my mind where I could have peace and feel safe.

We went back to his house had some more drinks and he rolled a joint. I had never tried drugs of any type before. He said try it. I said OK. Nothing happened. He said it was very good stuff. I tried another one. Nothing happened. That was my first and last encounter with drugs. They did nothing for me. A few hours later, early on Sunday morning, I had left Andrew's place and was driving northwards back to Hawick. I could hardly see, I was so drunk. I stopped the car along the way somewhere, parked up and fell into a stupor. I thought I was going to die and frankly I couldn't have cared less. I awoke in the early hours with a terrible head, feeling awful. I was parked across the pavement against a lamp-post outside a parade of shops in North London. Amazingly I was still alive. They had not found me! Whoever 'they', were!

I didn't know what to do now. I had to return to Hawick sometime or other. All my clothes and belongings were still in that apartment. Like a man stumbling along in a daze I drove up to Carlisle and went to a Catholic church for the first time in my life. I took mass and a circle of wafer from the priest. It seemed very religious and I felt uncomfortable. No one spoke to me. I checked into a hotel in Carlisle, no way was I going back to sleep in that flat of horrors in Hawick! In the evening I went to something called a Pentecostal church in Carlisle. The singing was good, they all seemed happy and they were very friendly. I tried to tell someone called a house group leader what had happened to me but I burst into tears. Several people put their arms around me and prayed for me. They seemed to understand what had happened to me and prayed against Satan and his demons. I felt a lot better. They told me that Jesus was the only answer. That night in the hotel I continued to be ill.

I was suffering from bright orange diarrhoea and my urine was a bright yellow-green colour. My face was still frozen and I felt very strange and ill. I was still very much afraid.

Next day I summoned up some courage from somewhere and drove to my office in Hawick and at 9 am 'phoned my born again Christian friend Steve. He and Katy had been on vacation in Devon and only just got back. That was why they were out when I called at their home on Saturday. When I described something of what had happened to me. Steve said, 'I think you need Jesus, don't you?'

'Yes,' I said quietly.

'What do you want to do?' he asked.

'Come down there,' I said.

'When?' he said.

'**Right now!**' I answered firmly, without the slightest hesitation or doubt.

Chapter 6

Jesus my Saviour and Deliverer

By Malcolm

T en minutes later I was driving down to Fleet again. I hadn't gone near the flat; my clothes and belongings would just have to wait! I arrived at Steve and Katy's house about 6.30 pm. After a meal Steve and I drove round to the house of someone called Malcolm Carter. Steve introduced him to me and said he was an elder of the King's Church, Aldershot. We went into his study and I told them both what had happened to me. After over an hour listening to my story Steve asked me if I wanted to ask Jesus into my life. I said, 'Yes,' and we prayed the prayer of salvation together. I confessed my sin, asked for forgiveness and asked the Lord Jesus Christ into my life. They hugged me and Steve said that the angels in heaven rejoice over just one sinner who repents and comes to Jesus. Then Steve said that he and Malcolm were going to pray in another tongue and they prayed over me in a strange language. They then cut me off from all the works of the enemy. That was the first time I heard anyone praying in tongues. It sounded weird.

It was 9.45 pm – **Monday 31st July 1989**.

The Lord had thrown me a lifeline and I grabbed it, without hesitation, with both hands! I was now a Christian! I was saved! It didn't feel that different, but I did seem to feel less afraid and more hopeful for the future.

On Monday 31st July 1989, I was to have begun the new job in South Wales as Chief Executive Officer for the Orange

Juice company on a salary of £30,000.00 plus car plus expenses etc. Instead I had gone to Fleet that day and given my life to the Lord! Next day Tuesday 1st August, I contacted the company and told them, that due to unforeseen circumstances I wouldn't be able to start until the following week. A few days later the company's offer of employment was withdrawn. Interestingly, their letter to me was dated – **Monday 31st July 1989**.

Later that week I went back to the flat in Hawick with considerable trepidation and quickly collected my gear. I had decided to move down to Fleet and Steve had offered to put me up for a while. The phone rang, I answered. It was Helen. She asked me why I hadn't called her.

I said that tarot cards were wrong and she screamed back angrily, 'It's that born again friend of yours, he's a bad influence. Don't listen to him or you'll be sorry!' I put the phone down. I never contacted or saw Helen or Bill again. Obviously if I'd known what I was getting myself into then I would never have gone near clairvoyants, mediums or the like. But I was ignorant and I couldn't see the danger right in front of my eyes. Satan is very clever, but Jesus describes him as the father of all lies. The Bible says many deceiving spirits have gone out into the world and are deceiving millions on the earth today. The medium, the astrologist, the channeller, the tarot reader, the fortune teller, they all derive their information from the same source – Satan and his fallen angels.

Familiar and Lying spirits

All the best lies have truth woven into them. When a spiritualist receives a message from 'the other side', he is actually receiving knowledge about a person or situation from a familiar spirit. The lie is more likely to be believed if it is wrapped up in outer layers of truth.

Thus a medium may know details about the person in front of them that no-one else could possibly know. The tarot cards, or star charts are only elaborate props, as is handling a ring or jewellery or whatever. These inanimate objects in themselves contain no power. The medium or whoever – does not in fact 'pick-up' anything at all from these things. Instead a familiar spirit projects thoughts and impressions directly into the mind of the 'go-between', who then relays them on to the 'client'. What is happening here is **counterfeit**. The original and only true 'gifts of the Spirit', are those bestowed by the **Holy Spirit to born again believers** as described in 1 Corinthians 12:4–10. The word of **wisdom**, the word of **knowledge**, the gift of **faith**, the gifts of **healings**, the working of **miracles**, the word of **prophecy**, the **discerning** of spirits, the gift of **tongues** and the **interpretation** of tongues, are all available to Spirit-filled Christians, but only in the name of **Jesus Christ of Nazareth**!

Exodus 7:8–12

> *'Then the* LORD *spoke to Moses and Aaron, saying, "When Pharoah speaks to you, saying, 'Show a miracle for yourselves,' then you shall say to Aaron, 'Take your rod and cast it before Pharoah, and let it become a serpent.'" So Moses and Aaron went in to Pharoah and they did so, just as the* LORD *commanded. And Aaron cast down his rod before Pharoah and before his servants, and it became a serpent. But when Pharoah also called the wise men and the sorcerers* (soothsayers); *so the magicians of Eygpt, they also did in like manner with their enchantments* (magic arts). *For every man threw down his rod, and they became serpents. But Aaron's rod swallowed up their rods.'*

These magicians were able to counterfeit or duplicate the plagues that Moses called down on Eygpt, even to the third plague. But on trying to bring forth the third plague, the plague of lice, they could not. The proponents of magic arts these days, the mediums, astrologers etc., are as deceived as their clients, they themselves believe the lie and do not recognise the power behind their 'gifts'. What exactly is the basis of the lie? What is the truth that the familiar and deceiving spirits are so desperate to conceal from their human dupes?

It is very simple:

> **Jesus Christ is the risen Son of God,
> come in the flesh to save mankind**.

These lying spirits will go to any lengths to cast a veil over the minds of men. The Bible says that all spirits should be tested and that any spirit that does not confess Jesus Christ as Lord is not from God.

Warning!

The children of Israel, were warned in Deuteronomy 18:9–12:

> *'When you come into the land that the LORD your God is giving you, you shall not learn to follow the abominations of those nations. There shall not be found among you anyone who makes his son or daughter pass through the fire* (fire-walking), *or one who practices witchcraft, or a soothsayer* (fortune teller), *or one who interprets omens, or a sorcerer, or one who conjures spells, or a medium, or a spiritist, or one who calls up the dead. For all who do these things are an abomination to the LORD and because of these abominations the LORD your God drives them out from before you.'*

I was ignorant of God's warning and followed some of these abominations. I later discovered that the occult comes in many forms and disguises, here are just a few of them:

Reflexolgy, Shiatsu Massage, Acupuncture, Astrology, Spiritualism, Toning, Eastern Martial Arts, Ancestor Worship, Fire-walking, Corn Circles, UFOs, Little Grey Aliens, Tall Fair Aliens, Tarot Cards, Shamenism, Paganism, King Arthur and the Druids, Freemasonry, Colourology, Palmistry, Graphology, Fairies, Pixies and Elves, Ghosts, Poltergeists, Levitation, Flying through the air, Spoon-bending, Star Signs, Zodiacs, Iridology, Crystalology, Re-incarnation, Red Indian spirits, Pyramidology, etc.

My advice to anyone reading this, involved in anything occult is:

Stop! Get out now!
Do not wait a moment longer!
Get on your knees right now
and pray out loud the prayer of salvation as follows:

Dear Lord Jesus,
I come to You now and confess my sins to You,
I declare publicly to principalities and powers
That I believe You are the risen son of the living
    God
That You died on Calvary's cross
That Your shed blood cleanses me from all my sins.
I Believe that the Father raised You on the third day
That through Your death and resurrection
I will have Eternal life.
Please wash me clean in Your precious blood from
    my involvement in ....
    (detail here your involvement)
    and cut me off from its effects.
I thank You Jesus that I am acceptable to the Father
    through my belief in You.
Thank You Lord.
Amen.

Seek out a Spirit-filled Christian Church and tell them what you have been involved in. Tell them you have prayed this prayer. Follow their advice.

So how is one supposed to tell what is right or wrong? God has made it very simple. Any practice, doctrine or belief that does not confess that Jesus Christ is the risen Lord, is not of God. There are only two powers in this Universe, God (Father, Son, and Holy Spirit) and Satan. There is no need for man to go looking to space and other planets for alien life forms, we are surrounded by them right here on earth! Ministering angels who bring God's people to salvation through Jesus Christ. Satan and the fallen angels (demons) who are diametrically opposed to the will of God.

I moved in to Steve's house in Fleet and later that week, on the Thursday evening I went with Steve and Katy to their house group. I was introduced to everyone. They all seemed to know me and made me feel very welcome. Steve explained later that he, Katy and the house group had been praying for me for many months before. They had known all about my involvement with Bill and Helen and had interceded with the Lord on my behalf. Such is the power of intercessory prayer! My special thanks then is due to Steve and Katy, Martin and Sandra, Dave and Maureen, Sarah, Sean and Sara, Mark and Sue. On Sunday we went to the King's Church, Aldershot. The singing was wonderful – praise and worship they called it.

The whole of the building was decorated in different shades of green: chairs, ceiling, carpets, walls. I felt that I'd come home. I felt a bit nervous. But I felt safe. Sanctuary at last!

Gradually I began to recover. I had lost two stones and I began to gain weight. The diahorrea and green urine cleared up. I moved into a quiet bungalow shared by Sara, Les, and Roy. I found myself in a totally different environment in the space of only a few days. No-one swore, they prayed and read the Bible a lot. People were genuinely kind to each other. Soon it was time for me to collect my girls for the weekend. Adrienne and Winona liked my new home and the church. Everyone was very kind to them. There were lots of children their own age. Adrienne was eight and Winona six. We were befriended by a lovely Christian couple, Sue and Jeff Fisher and their family who became very good friends. Sue Fisher was an excellent cook and when my girls were down from the Midlands, Sunday lunch times were a special treat.

I still had a problem with fear though. One Saturday night in particular there was a lot of aircraft noise, which I was later to find out came from the nearby Ministry of Defence base at Farnborough. I somehow became extremely fearful and my mind imagined all sorts of alien craft hovering above looking for me. Strange thoughts invaded my brain. I was a fake, an imposter, I would be found out sooner or later. I would never be accepted, soon I would be exposed and thrown out of the church. In abject terror I lay awake all night, repeating over and over again the Lord's Prayer. Next morning in the King's Church after the praise and worship a visiting lady from South Africa announced she had a 'word' for someone in fear and spoke out from the back:

> 'Do not be afraid, the Lord your God is with you, He will shelter you under the shadow of His wings!'

I knew that word was for me and that God was talking to me. I was greatly comforted. Later that day glancing through my Bible, for the first time I discovered the marvellous Psalm 91.

Chapter 7

Divine Reassurance

by Malcolm

'He who dwells in the secret place of the Most High
Shall abide under the shadow of the Almighty.
I will say of my LORD, "He is my refuge and my fortress;
My God, in Him I will trust."
Surely He shall deliver you from the snare of the fowler
And from the perilous pestilence.
He shall cover you with His feathers
And under His wings you shall take refuge:
His truth shall be your shield and buckler
You shall not be afraid of the terror by night,
Nor of the arrow that flies by day,
Nor of the pestilence that walks in darkness,
Nor of the destruction that lays waste at noonday.

A thousand may fall at your side,
And ten thousand at your right hand;
But it shall not come near you.
Only with your eyes shall you look,
And see the reward of the wicked.

Because you have made the LORD, who is my refuge,
Even the Most High, your habitation,
No evil shall befall you,
Nor shall any plague come near your dwelling;
For He shall give His angels charge over you,
To keep you in all your ways.

They shall bear you up in their hands,
Lest you dash your foot against a stone.
You shall tread upon the lion and the cobra,
The young lion and the serpent you shall trample underfoot.

Because he has set his love on Me, therefore I will deliver
    him;
I will set him on high, because he has known My name.
He shall call upon Me, and I will answer Him;
I will be with him in trouble;
I will deliver him and honour him.
With long life I will satisfy him,
And show him my salvation.'   (Psalm 91)

T here couldn't have been a more fitting or apt scripture
    for my situation and the satanic oppression I was under
than these marvellous verses. Something happened deep
within me. A sure feeling in my spirit that every word was
true and that no harm could befall me if I continued to,
'abide under the shadow of the Almighty!' The terror and fear
left me. I could sleep soundly in my bed once more.

I began to learn more about the Christian life. The
language of faith. The music, the praise and worship. Books,
tapes, teaching. A whole new sub-culture that I never knew
existed was revealed to me. But I thought that I could live as
I had before, only with the new tag of Christian attached to
me. Little did I know the Lord! I may have become a
Christian but I hadn't basically changed. Outwardly I
seemed OK, but inside I was full of anger and bitterness
towards my wife. I knew little of righteousness. Derek Brown
the pastor at the King's Church, was a brilliant teacher. He
made the Word come alive. I studied and read about
forgiveness and agape love. I gradually began to adjust to
my new life. No more night clubs, bad language, sexual
immorality. For the first time in my life I experienced
platonic relationships with women.

I committed several notable *faux pas* in my first few weeks
as a Christian. I remember a lunch one Sunday when I
was living with Roy, Les and Sara in Fleet. Roy suggested we
take bread and wine before eating our meal and duly

brought in from the kitchen a glass of wine and a piece of bread on a small plate, both of which he placed in front of me. After he said a short prayer, Roy asked me to take the bread and wine. To the astonishment of the others, I gobbled up the piece of bread and drained the glass in one gulp. For a while nobody said anything. Then I said, 'Aren't you people having any?'

Roy quietly explained, 'Malcolm, you're supposed to take a small piece of bread and a sip of wine and pass it to your neighbour!'

I had obtained some temporary training consultancy work in Aldershot. I had £10,000.00 or so in my personal bank account, a BMW 5 Series car, business was doing OK, so I was able to keep up the maintenance payments for my children and continue to pay into the various pension and insurance investment plans that I had started several years earlier. I began to try and expand my business.

Christian life was OK. A born again believer was entitled to prosperity – right? At least that was what many of my new brothers and sisters were experiencing. Why not me? I obtained a licence to start a recruitment agency. I met a Christian about my own age at the King's Church who had recently experienced the failure of his own business. He joined me in consultancy with a view to getting the recruitment side off the ground. Unfortunately he had lots of personal problems and we parted company a couple of months later. It was not a happy experience. I had been warned about this man but I thought he would be OK. I began to learn that just because someone believed in Jesus, that didn't mean that they were necessarily living right. I went through a period when I believed that I was totally undeserving of God's salvation – that I could never measure up. I didn't fully understand God's infinite grace towards us and that I was fully **justified and made righteous** through the precious blood of the Lamb.

Baptism in Water

After completing six weeks of Wednesday evenings on a course entitled *Committed for Life*, I was ready to be baptised in water, four months after I was saved. The teaching course was invaluable. About twenty new Christians met each week in one of the meeting rooms in the King's Church, Aldershot. There various pastors and elders took us through the basics of the Christian faith. I learned in detail exactly what it meant to be delivered, *'from the power of darkness and translated into the Kingdom of the Son of His love.'* I learned exactly who Satan was – the adversary, the accuser, the tempter, the murderer, the father of lies, the prince of the power of the air, with the whole world in his grip. I learned about the power of darkness, about Satan's rebellion and his eviction from heaven along with a third of the angels. I learned what had happened to me and what exactly I had been up against. I learned that Satan and his demons were extremely danger-ous, far above mankind in power and intelligence. I learned how Adam the first man lost his dominion and authority over God's creation and how God so loved the world that He gave His only Son to save mankind from the fate already decreed for Satan and his demons.

I learned that there was only one man in the whole of creation, the entire Universe, who is qualified and is not only able to overcome Satan and all his host, but has already done so on the Cross at Calvary. The man Jesus Christ. I learned that it is only through our belief in the LORD Jesus Christ and the authority we have in Him that we can overcome the wicked one. I learned what it meant to be born-again of the Holy Spirit. I learned of the significance of water baptism and how it is important that we *'repent and are baptised in the name of Jesus Christ for the remission of sins.'* That baptism represents the burial of our old selves in the grave with Jesus, and that when we arise from the water we are raised in the 'newness of life.' So on 17th November 1989, I was baptised in the tank of lukewarm water at the King's Church. On emerging from the pool I was pleased and excited, but I didn't feel that different.

The Gift of Tongues and Praying in the Spirit

About three days later I was sitting relaxing in the bath (my favourite form of relaxation), just praising the Lord for my deliverance and salvation, when some strange sounds came out of my mouth: 'Shama Lama Ro'sh!'

I was amazed. I had heard others speaking in tongues and now I was doing the same! I kept repeating them over and over again. A few days later again whilst relaxing in the bath, 'Keriente, Abba, Shaba' Shabbat!'

I continued to receive a further nine words this way over the next week, always three at a time: 'Soto Shavak al'Hava' – 'Sundara Shavak al'Hava' – 'Baruch a'chaim Hava.'

A few months later I was praying out loud these words when a Christian friend, Nick exclaimed, 'You're praying in Hebrew!'

I had never even heard the Hebrew language spoken. Nick was studying Hebrew and roughly translated what he could. Apparently I was asking God, 'Why has this net been cast over my head, Father?'

I was also apparently making some sort of solemn oath. The Hebrew word *'Shaba'*, means 'to swear allegiance through a binding oath; to give one's unbreakable word that one will faithfully perform a promised deed.' Then something about a particular weekend, which Nick could not make out, and then the last phrase, 'Blessed is the life to come!'

As far as I can understand the net cast over my head refers to the experience I had in Scotland when I was attacked by demonic powers.

(Tongues are a heavenly language given by the Holy Spirit, meant to be spoken rather than read. In my description of these words, the spelling here is phonetic rather than literally correct. The language may even be an ancient dialect such as Aramaic, which is still spoken today according to Mrs Bishop John Stanley, who kindly informed me of this fact when she read the manuscript for this book.)

There is much we simply do not know about the realm of the Spirit. My own experience would seem to suggest that once our own spirit is energised by God's Holy Spirit, our spirit is able to communicate directly with God, even bypassing our human minds in the process.

Chapter 8

A Childhood Wound Cleaned
and Healed

by Malcolm

O ne day I went down to Bristol to collect my parents
who were coming to stay in Fleet with me for the
weekend. They now seemed perfectly normal, or rather
it was me that was now perfectly normal. My thoughts
and mind no longer subject to interference by demonic
oppression.

> *'For God has not given us a spirit of fear, but of power and of
> love and of a sound mind.'* (2 Timothy 1:7)

I had a party that night and introduced my parents to my
new friends and took them to the King's Church next day. I
thought they would think it a strange kind of church, but
they loved it, particularly the praise and worship. My father
especially was moved and there were tears in his eyes as he
sang and praised the Lord. A few months later I got a phone
call from Steve Hannington, who was recovering from an
operation to remove his tonsils. He told me that he had been
in the bathroom shaving that morning when the Lord spoke
to him: 'Kneel!' a voice said.

Steve knelt. 'Tell Malcolm to go home!' said the voice.

I explained to Steve that I didn't have a home anymore,
except my parent's home in Bristol. 'That must be it then!'
he croaked, 'You're to go home!'

I phoned my parents that night and arranged to stay with

them for the weekend. I arrived on the Friday night in time
for tea. As we sat at the table my mother asked how Steve
was. I explained that he was recovering from having his
tonsils removed and she began to look very sheepish. She
recalled that I'd had my own tonsils removed when I was
four years old and that she had been very upset over the
matter. She explained that neither she nor my father had
the heart to tell me what was going to happen, and that they
thought that the best thing would be to say nothing. She
said that she felt dreadful leaving me in that Hospital
without saying a word, and had been feeling guilty ever
since.

I said that I hadn't been exactly pleased myself, but that
after all this time it really didn't matter. That was all that was
said on the subject. But I felt that I had been shown things
from my mother's point of view and that I was to forgive her.
I prayed later in the privacy of my room and forgave my
mother and asked the Lord's forgiveness for holding a grudge
against her. I later felt like a weight had been removed from
me, something that had been troubling me a long time. It
had taken nearly forty years. But God had removed it from
me! Our relationship still is relatively undemonstrative, but I
know I have been set free and those the Lord sets free are free
indeed! I understood then that the devil had used my
unforgiveness toward my mother and that had been at the
root of my distrust of women all my life. It is only when we
come to know the Lord Jesus Christ and we ourselves receive
forgiveness, that we can forgive others. It is not possible
without the Lord. For we cannot give what we have not
received.

Baptism with the Spirit

In the early months of 1990, I was having difficulties seeing
my children. My wife and I were not yet divorced and I
believed that they were in moral danger by her casual
association with men. I sought to obtain custody without
success and she denied me access for three months. I was
very angry and bitter and extremely depressed. I was still
having strange sensations in my body as I lay in bed at

night. Sometimes I could feel something pressing down hard on my chest. But this time I wasn't afraid, just angry. These sensations generally disappeared on my praying the Lord's prayer. One evening about three months after I was saved, I was round at Steve Hannington's house bemoaning my lot and we argued about my actions in attempting to obtain custody. Steve felt I should not have instigated proceedings but trusted in the Lord to sort it out. I got angry and left their house in a temper about 10.30 pm and went straight home to bed, my spirit feeling like lead within me. I cried out to God for help.

As soon as I got into bed, I felt the most powerful waves of energy begin to surge through my body. I sat up and was thrown out of bed onto the floor. I hurriedly switched the light on but could see nothing. Eventually I returned to bed and immediately the most wonderful intense tingling sensation began in my feet and gradually spread up through my body. The only way to describe it, is that it felt like a warm jacuzzi, but somehow on the inside of my body! Throughout my arms, legs and trunk right up to my neck. The feeling was **fantastic**, all my cares, bitterness, resentment, anger seemed to be washed away. It felt like the Lord had wrapped His arms around me, which of course He had. This powerful anointing, this indescribable physical sensation stayed with me as I drifted off into a marvellous deep sleep and when I woke up three hours later, there it was again! It had never left me, even in my sleep. It eventually subsided about 8 am as I arose to go to the office. Next day, I apologised to Steve on the 'phone and described what had happened the previous night.

'What time did this happen?' he enquired. 'About 11 pm,' I replied.

'That's exactly the time Katy and I prayed that you should receive the Baptism with the Spirit!' he exclaimed.

Every night for the next six months I was bathed in the gentle loving power of the Holy Spirit. I experienced no further visitations from demonic powers, all the oppression went. I cried out to the Lord to change me. I hated my old self and wanted nothing more to do with it. 'Change me,' I cried, 'whatever the cost!'

In dreams, the Holy Spirit took me back to my childhood, and showed me in great detail, events where my spirit had been hurt and bruised by the actions of others and where there was unforgiveness. He showed me too where I had caused damage to myself and others by my own sinful actions. Whole years flashed before my eyes in a moment of time. A particular year revealed a particular hurt. He showed me the root of my distrust of women – the traumatic hospital experience when I was a child of four, long forgotten, but buried and still active, deep in my subconscious. Sometimes I wept copiously and awoke to find the pillows soaked with my tears. Sometimes I laughed like a hyena, full of a happiness and joy, beyond description. No therapist or psychiatrist could have matched that work of the Holy Spirit. I was receiving deep therapy from my Creator. I was like an office filing cabinet and because He knew everything there was to know about me, He could go straight to the right file, open up the contents and show me exactly what had happened in my life. But I had to be willing to face whatever He revealed to me, good or bad and be prepared to repent and ask forgiveness or to forgive others.

Soon I received a calmness, a tranquillity, deep in my inner being that I had never known before. The Shalom Peace of God. I can honestly say an atom bomb could have been detonated next to me and I would not have been disturbed in the least. This must have been what the early Christians experienced when they faced the lions in the Roman arena and to martyrs through the centuries as they faced death. I consulted my pastor, Derek, about what I was experiencing. He listened attentively and after careful consideration he concluded that I was receiving God's grace. I believe that in addition to deep inner healing, I was also being prepared for what was to come, for during that period I underwent many trials.

A woman came to work for me who was extremely good looking, divorced and great fun. She was not a Christian and teased me a lot about my beliefs. After a few weeks our relationship deepened. I was round at her house one night, we had just finished our Chinese takeaway, when she came and sat on my knee. She began to partially undress and then laid on the floor.

'Why don't you come and take her?' she said in a familiar voice.

I recognised the spirit within her. Being a new Christian at that time I didn't know what to do, or how to get rid of that spirit. All I knew was that I was being severely tempted. But I had learned my lesson through my terrifying experience with Helen! No way was I going to be anything but celibate. I was not going to open myself up again to the demonic. I merely smiled politely, declined the offer, and immediately left.

I believe that the Word tells us not to indulge in sexual intercourse outside marriage for good reason. Not because God is against sex, or that He does not want us to enjoy ourselves. After all it was He that invented sex in the first place! No, it is because it is not just a physical experience, but also the joining together of one spirit to another. In the original male and female relationship that God designed, God is meant to be at the centre. The three-corded strand that is not easily broken. If this relationship exists in a casual way, without God, then it is open to demonic influence and sometimes as in my own personal experience, by demonic spirits. By sleeping around as I did and disobeying God's law, not only was I risking the physical consequences of my immoral behaviour, such as a sexually transmitted disease, but also the spiritual consequences of joining my spirit to that of another and contracting in effect, 'Spiritual AIDS.'

In sleeping with someone who was a practioner of occult 'magic' who had opened herself up to demonic possession, hence the multiple 'personalities', I was opening myself up to the same danger. It was only through God's grace and mercy towards me through His son Jesus Christ that I was able to receive salvation, deliverance and healing from the effects of sin on my body, mind, soul and spirit. I know what I am talking about here without the slightest shadow of doubt, for I have experienced God's wonderful love and the power of His Spirit towards 'the objects of His mercy' at first hand, for myself.

The Man in the Pub!

On one occasion I and my friend Nick Kannenmeyer went to a Marilyn Baker concert at the King's Church with this woman and a friend of hers, who professed to be a white witch. They found the concert uncomfortable and left during the interval for a drink at the pub across the road. After the concert ended we all went to a nearby pub for a drink.

'This is going to be challenged,' I said to Nick as we got out of the car, 'Satan does not want us taking his own to Christian concerts!'

We went into the pub, ordered our drinks and sat down. Immediately a young man, a complete stranger in his twenties, came over.

'I suppose you have been down at that King's Church,' he said, 'You want to keep away from that place; full of Americans just wanting to take your money and telling you a pack of lies.'

He continued to berate the church in a very aggressive manner, blaspheme against the Lord and try to start a fight. Nick and I prayed in tongues under our breaths. I looked over at the table where he had been sitting. The girl he was with, sat motionless like a statue, staring straight ahead, holding her drink to her mouth, but she was not drinking. It was as if she had been frozen solid. After fifteen minutes or so of this haranguing he went back to his table and sat down. His girlfriend came 'back to life' sipped her drink and continued talking as though nothing had happened. When we got home that night Nick said that he had never seen anything like it before and could now understand some of my experiences which I had described to him.

Two nights later he rushed in, just back from a session at the Aldershot artificial ski slope.

'Guess what!' he cried. 'Who do you think I talked to at the ski slope?'

'No idea,' I replied.

'The man in the pub!' he said. 'He was quite friendly, so I asked him what he meant the other night, and he didn't have a clue what I was talking about! He didn't know a thing about it and doesn't even remember talking to us!'

'Thursday'

During 1990, approximately five months after I was saved, the famous English evangelist and healer Ian Andrews visited the King's Church with his wife. I was impressed with the graphic detail Ian used to describe the trial and the crucifixion of our Lord Jesus Christ. His description of the terrible scourging that Jesus underwent brought many to tears, including myself. His description of the Roman scourge, a horrendous instrument of torture, a many-stranded whip with sharp pieces of lead and glass attached to the end of the strands and how it was applied to the back of its victim was terrifying. Thirty-nine strokes were applied to the Lord's back with the full strength of a strong man behind each blow.

In a typical scourging, after a few strokes the skin was flayed off the back and the separate leather whip strands of the scourge wrapped themselves around the rib cage. A scourging of thirty-nine strokes would have laid the flesh bare, exposing both the spinal column and part of the rib cage.

Thus the scripture, Psalm 22 verse 17, a crucifixion scripture written 1100 years before the birth of Jesus, was fulfilled:

'I can count all my bones.
They look and stare at me.'

After this the Roman soldiers took turns to pound the face of Jesus into a bloody pulp and then rammed the crown of thorns onto his head. I have visited Israel and seen the type of thorn which commonly grows there. It is a tough plant which closely resembles barbed wire, with many vicious spikes exceeding one inch in length. The pain of this torture alone must have been dreadful.

By this the scripture was fufilled:

'So His visage was marred more than any man.'
(Isaiah 52:14)

Several people accepted Jesus into their lives at this meeting and Ian and his wife received many words of knowledge during the healing time of their ministry.

Their knowledge was uncanny, Ian would speak out names and conditions and diagnoses and he would lay hands on those people in the name of the Lord and they would receive healing. Towards the end of the evening, Ian said that he had received a word of knowledge the like of which he had never received or experienced before.

He said, 'It makes no sense to me but perhaps it makes sense to someone here. The Lord has given me the word "**Thursday.**"' Immediately something within me quickened and I knew this word was for me. I went forward for prayer. Ian asked me if I understood the word and whether I believed it had come from God. I replied that I **knew** beyond doubt it had come from God and that the word was exclusively for me. He then prayed a prayer over me and told me that I had been set free and healed! I was overjoyed, I had confirmation that the Lord had been **with** me during that terrible week in Hawick prior to my being saved and that he was with me still!

Jesus Christ of Nazareth, the Suffering Servant

There are some twenty-six separate Old Testament prophecies concerning the prediction that the Messiah would be crucified. Some point directly to the crucifixion – some to the events surrounding the cross. Jesus Christ, the Messiah is the only one to fulfil all these prophecies, some of which were written 1100 years before His birth.

- The seed of the woman shall bruise Satan's head and Satan shall bruise His heel.   (Genesis 3:15)

- As Moses lifted up the serpent, so I shall be lifted up.
                                                        (Numbers 21:8–9)

- *'And the rulers take counsel together,*
  Against the Lord *and His Anointed.'*   (Psalm 2:2)

- His Holy one would not see corruption.   (Psalm 16:10)

- Jesus cried out, *'My God, My God, Why hast thou forsaken Me?'*
                                                        (Psalm 22:1)

– They laughed scorned and reviled Him.   (Psalm 22:7)

– They said, 'He trusted in God, let him deliver him now!'
(Psalm 22:8)

– *'For dogs have surrounded Me;*
  The assembly of the wicked has enclosed Me.
  They pierced My hands and My feet.'   (Psalm 22:16)

– *'I can count all My bones.*
  They look and stare at Me.'   (Psalm 22:17)

– *'They divide My garments among them,*
  And for My clothing they cast lots.'   (Psalm 22:18)

– *'He guards all his bones;*
  Not one of them is broken.'   (Psalm 34:20)

– Jesus was betrayed by a friend.   (Psalm 41:9)

– *'They also gave me gall for my food,*
  And for my thirst they gave me vinegar to drink.'
(Psalm 69:21)

– *'Let his* (Judas) *days be few,*
  And let another (Matthias) *take his office.'*   (Psalm 109:8)

– *'I gave My back to those who struck Me,*
  And My cheeks to those who plucked out the beard;
  I did not hide My face from shame and spitting.'
(Isaiah 50:6)

– *' . . . He was wounded for our transgressions,*
  He was bruised for our iniquities;
  The chastisement for our peace was upon Him,
  And by His stripes we are healed.'   (Isaiah 53:5)

– *' . . . the* LORD *laid on Him the iniquity of us all.'*
(Isaiah 53:6)

– He was led like a lamb to the slaughter but remained
  silent.   (Isaiah 53:7)

– He was with the wicked and the rich in His death and
  burial.   (Isaiah 53:9)

– He was made an offering for sin.   (Isaiah 53:10)

- *'Because He poured out His soul unto death,*
  And He was numbered with the transgressors,
  And He bore the sin of many,
  And made intercession for the transgressors.' (Isaiah 53:12)

- The sun was darkened at the sixth hour.   (Amos 8:9)

- Jesus rode into Jerusalem on a donkey.   (Zechariah 9:9)

- Jesus was betrayed for thirty pieces of silver – a potters
  field was bought with the money.   (Zechariah 11:12)

- *'. . . they will look on Me whom they have pierced.'*
                                            (Zechariah 12:10)

- The shepherd was struck and the sheep scattered.
                                            (Zechariah 13:7)

> **'For Jews request a sign, and Greeks seek after wisdom;**
> **but we preach Christ crucified, to the Jews a stumbling**
> **block and to the Greeks foolishness, but to those who**
> **are called, both Jews and Greeks, Christ the power of**
> **God and the wisdom of God. Because the foolishness**
> **of God is wiser than men, and the weakness of God is**
> **stronger than men.'**   (1 Corinthians 1:22–25)

If you think the twenty-six separate prophetic references
to Jesus' crucifixion and death in the Old Testament are
amazing, then consider this – they are multiplied by a factor
of thirteen, when one considers the over **three hundred**
New Testament scriptural references to His Second Coming –
only this time not as a suffering servant, but as the all
conquering, King of kings and Lord of lords!

Marion

Several months later during that summer of 1990, Pastor
Derek Brown in a Sunday morning meeting said that the
Lord had given him the name, 'Marion', for someone in
the congregation and that Marion was this person's sister-in-
law and that they should come forward for prayer as the
Lord wanted to deal with a situation. I knew that this was a

word for me, but I didn't go forward. Later, I spent the whole afternoon sunbathing in the warm summer sun and wept piteously for several hours. At the end of that period I felt that a weight had been lifted off my shoulders and I felt refreshed and restored. Marion was my ex-wife's sister and I had felt hatred towards her and blamed her in part for helping to turn my wife, her sister, against me. But in His infinite mercy toward me, the Lord lifted all those negative feelings about her from my heart and pulled out the root of bitterness. Praise the Lord!

Chapter 9

Out of the Frying Pan into the Fire

by Malcolm

Having reached the end of my temporary consultancy contract I decided to try and find a permanent executive position, despite being wary about getting back onto the corporate treadmill. I had been made redundant four times in the past seventeen years and knew that there was no such thing as job security in the modern business world. I applied for a few positions and received an offer of employment as a Sales Manager for the recently formed Red Telephone Company. This was an Australian operation that was successful on that Continent in the business of private pay phones. The salary offer was only equivalent to that which I had been earning six years previously, but they supplied a car and made promises of high commission earnings in addition to the basic salary so I decided to accept the position offered. I commenced my job with the Red Telephone Company in August and for three months worked hard to build the business in the South London region. I recruited eight new sales people and most of my time was spent in training and the development of their potential. This investment in time and energy began to pay off and the business flowed in. It was beginning to look as though I could re-establish myself as a successful Sales Manager. Praise the Lord! However, all this initial success was about to be brought to a sudden and premature end.

On 1st November 1990, I was driving to a training meeting I had organised in a Hotel near Croydon, Surrey and as I stopped in a queue of traffic at a busy road junction, a car drove into the back of my vehicle at high speed and with considerable force. I sustained whiplash and concussion injuries and was unable to complete my day's work. Over the next few days I suffered memory loss, blurred vision and severe headaches. These continued for several weeks, during which time I was unable to work. At the end of December having been off work, due to the accident, for eight weeks, the Company terminated my employment. I felt yet again that the rug had been pulled from beneath my feet. For the next nine months I had no income. Remarkably, I had not been driving the company's vehicle on the day of the accident, but my own BMW 5 Series which I had purchased a year earlier.

This car had been owned by the Mars confectionery group based in Slough, West London and had been converted to tow a large trailer by having special reinforcing steel sections fitted to the rear of the car inside the boot (USA: trunk). Had I been driving the Company's own car, a smaller, rather lightly constructed hatchback, my injuries may have been much more severe. Amazingly, the only reason I was driving the reinforced BMW that day was because the Red Telephone Company car had inexplicably refused to start the previous day. Interestingly enough, the Vauxhall main dealer in Aldershot could find nothing wrong with it and were at a loss to explain why it had malfunctioned! I knew exactly what had happened, The Lord kept me from greater harm by ensuring that I was driving a larger and safer car that day! A car that had **additional** protection against rear end collision. Further, my own car insurance policy provided for the recovery of un-insured losses.

That meant that the insurance company would foot the bill for pursuing my claim against the other driver's insurance, through the courts, to a maximum of £50,000 worth of legal costs. The Red Telephone's company vehicles insurance policy did not have this provision and had I been driving their car, not only could my injuries have been more serious, I would have been unable to pursue my case through the courts. This has proved to be a protracted and fraught procedure as at the time of writing this account, some seven years after the accident, my claim has still not yet been settled!

Over the next nine months I completely ran out of money and was on the verge of bankruptcy. I was unable to maintain payments to my credit card companies and a couple of bank loans which became due. I lost all the money which I had paid into pension and insurance and medical-care plans for many years. I received County Court summonses for non-payment of arrears and was black-listed by every credit agency in the land. I was powerless to resolve my financial situation by my own efforts and had to throw myself entirely on the Lord's mercy. During this period the lease on the bungalow which I shared with Sara and Nick came to an end. We were all to part company, and go our separate ways. I decided regrettably, that I had no alternative but to return home to Bristol and throw myself on my parent's charity. When I informed Sara on the day we moved out of the bungalow of my intentions in this regard, she became a different person! Sara was standing on a chair cleaning a curtain rail when she thundered in a voice of great authority, 'The Lord says to you, Malcolm, that obedience is better than sacrifice and that you are to stay here, in this area and continue in the church that He has placed you in!'

Nick and I stood speechless, both realising that this was not the Sara that we both were familiar with, but that this was most definitely a word from the Lord. So, later that day, I went round to the house of a fellow Church member, Joe Lucas who lived in nearby Farnham, to view the room to rent he had advertised in the church notices.

A Bishop's Prophecy

The room was small and bare, a single put-u-up bed with no cupboard space or wardrobe. I would have to hang my clothes on coat hangers from a picture rail, but it was cheap and in a Christian house so I took it. I told Joe of my dreadful financial position and he didn't seem too bothered. I had taken a temporary job helping to set up a 'Mineral Water to your Home' delivery service in the Aldershot area and I had to work long hours, some sixty per week in fact, for the grand sum of £100.00! That night at 8 pm as I moved my belongings in, I opened the lounge door and was confronted with the sight and sound of some thirty born-again Christians praising and worshipping the Lord in full voice. I had walked into a meeting of the Farnham Riverside Church who were having their meeting in Joe's house that evening. Their guest speaker was Bishop David Pytches who was laying hands on people who then promptly fell on the floor. I joined in with everyone else in the praise and worship and when David Pytches, whom I had never heard of, came to me, he made the sign of the cross with his index finger on the palms of my hands and informed me that, 'God is going to use you greatly in the ministry of healing.'

I continued to struggle financially for a few more months until I completely ran out of money. I borrowed a friend's estate car and sold practically all that I possessed at a local car boot sale, in order to pay the rent and buy food. At the end of July, **all** the money I possessed in the world was four pence! I had received words directly from the Lord that I was going to be earning a living doing something to do with water. So when the temporary water delivery job, came to an end, I thought I had got it all wrong.

That hot July in 1991 I had reached the end of my resources. I had no money, no job and since the accident not much prospect of getting one. My insurance claim against the other driver was likely to drag on for several years.

'Lord,' I cried out,'You who made the heavens and earth, why don't You help me? What have I done to deserve this?'

In frustration and anger I shook my fist at the heavens and declared, 'Give me a call when You've got some time to spare for me, and **maybe** I'll answer!'

Chapter 10

Blessed in Business
by Malcolm

S oon I was completely indifferent as to whether God answered me or not. I lay on my sun-lounger in the garden for three weeks and concentrated on getting a good tan. I was not angry or bitter, I steadfastly continued to go to the King's Church and praised and worshipped the Lord with the rest – I was just indifferent to whether God was going to help me or not! However at the end of three weeks of this, I went to see our pastor, Derek Brown. I had no money for the bus, so on the hottest day of the summer, I had to walk the two or three miles to his office in the church. As I explained my predicament and how I had no money even for my bus fare, Derek suddenly said, 'The Lord's going to bless you in business!'

I was flabbergasted. 'You must be joking,' I said.

'No,' said Derek, 'The Holy Spirit is talking to me now, and the Lord is going to bless you in business, I don't know how, but that's what He is going to do!'

With that, the interview seemed over. Derek is a man of few words on these occasions, and I soon found myself trudging back along the road home. At least he could have lent me the fare for a bus, I thought! Several Christian friends told me that I should be claiming State Benefits – housing payments, unemployment allowances, that sort of thing. But I refused to even consider it! He was meant to be my provider, the mighty Jehovah Jireh – not Jehovah Giro! (A Giro is a welfare money order.) At this time my ex-wife was enjoying rapid almost meteoric promotion with her employer. Exactly at the same time as my fortunes went crashing down hers went soaring up. (Although she laughs me to scorn on this, I know God undertook for her.) My children were being well provided for, so I didn't have to worry on that score.

No, this was between God and me! I had been tithing faithfully since I was saved, even when I had virtually no money. I knew that He would have to provide for me somehow, He said so in His word – and it's **His** word, not mine!

'And test Me in this now,' He says in Malachi 3:10 concerning tithes and offerings. (The only area in which we are allowed to test or prove God.)

Nick Kannenmeyer came round later that week and in the middle of a time of prayer he suddenly exclaimed, 'I've got a picture of two golden angels nine feet high going before you with two huge swords and sweeping all the works of the enemy out of your path!'

Peter Smith was the other tenant who lived in Joe's house. He had been a Christian for twenty years and went to the Riverside Church in Farnham. Peter didn't have much time for people who went to the King's Church and thought that they were 'a bit off the wall'. Peter had a carpet cleaning machine and seemed to do odd bits of work now and again. One day he asked me if I would give him a hand to clean the carpets in a large house in the village of Seale, near Farnham and promised to pay me £50.00 for the day's work. I readily agreed. I desperately needed the money. The work went well, although I did most of it and I was amazed at how clean the carpets were at the end of the process, during which we used gallons and gallons of guess what – water!

I thought to myself that it would be easier to clean office carpets with less furniture to move about and larger areas of carpet, economy of scale etc. I asked Peter whether he had thought of approaching companies with his service. He replied that he had thought of it, but was rather intimidated by people in suits. I said that it was worth having a go at and he agreed that I would carry out some marketing for him along those lines. The first week I visited almost every business premises in Farnham, leaving a sales-letter which I had devised and produced on my word processor at home. Unfortunately there was not the slightest bit of interest. We prayed about the matter and I felt the Lord tell me to, 'cast my net on the other side of the boat.'

The following week I journeyed to nearby Camberley and walked around a modern business park with large office blocks. The very first company I approached, Toshiba, showed interest and we arranged to carry out a demonstration clean in their staff restaurant. The carpet tiles had not been cleaned properly by their existing cleaning company and were very dirty and greasy. However our system was more powerful and efficient and soon the tiles looked like new. The Toshiba Facilities Manager, Kevin Smith was delighted.

'Can you get the rest of the building looking like this?' he asked.

We said we could and we got down to negotiating a regular maintenance contract. During the interview with Kevin terms were agreed and he said, 'Have you recently started in business?'

We said we had, and he replied, 'Then we'd better pay you in advance, is three months OK?'

Peter and I looked at each other in amazement and replied that it was indeed, OK! (I discovered later we were the only supplier that Toshiba paid in advance!)

Afterwards in the car park outside, we sat praising the Lord for his kindness and wonderful provision. During those early weeks the business really took off, so much so that in one month we invoiced more business than Peter had done in the whole of the previous year. New contracts just flooded in. We obtained cleaning work with American Express, Royal Life Insurance, IBM etc. We were able to invest in new equipment, new and better marketing campaigns and the future was looking pretty good.

Peter though, did not have a head for figures and eventually turned the business finances over to me. I wasn't too concerned because I had been just as bad myself many years earlier. I employed a proper bookkeeper and took responsibility for the financial and marketing side of the business, whilst Peter concentrated on purely operational matters.

Helena

The first time I met Helena, I offered to escort her to the Yacht Club July barbecue of which Joe Lucas was a member. We arranged to follow Joe down the M3 to a farm near Winchester where the barbecue was to be held. Following Joe on the motorway was easier said than done as he drove at a frightening pace. Although I increased my speed to 80 miles an hour plus I could not keep up with him and he was soon lost from sight. Helena and I never found the farm and instead decided to eat at a country pub in Micheldever, Hampshire. Joe later professed complete innocence of his speed of departure and could not understand why we had been unable to keep up with him. When I had moved to Joe Lucas's house in Farnham I met several members of the Riverside Church there and Helena Wilkinson was one of the Christians I met. She was a friend of Peter Smith's and we met several times socially and at church gatherings.

I discovered that she was a Christian author and lectured on dietary and eating disorders, having overcome anorexia in her own life. Adrienne and Winona liked her and shared her interest in horses.

One evening when we were all having a meal in the Pizza Piazza in Farnham, my youngest daughter Winona announced in a voice so loud that the whole restaurant could hear, 'My Dad's not bad for forty-four is he, Helena?'

I quickly changed the conversation back to horses.

Helena was a lovely young woman with a great sense of humour. She and I were just friends, and although we all got on very well, she struck me as being a very private person. She has a wonderful testimony and she has written several excellent books telling her story including, *Puppet on a String* and *Snakes and Ladders*. Well worth a read!

One evening we had arranged to cycle to a pub outside Farnham and I borrowed Joe's racing bicycle and turned up at her house. We cycled off together but I soon found that the twenty-year interval since I last rode a bicycle began to take its toll, so much so that when we came to a particularly steep hill, I ran out of puff and had to dismount and wearily push the bike up the hill. Helena was ahead of me by several hundred yards and returned a few minutes later to discover what the problem was. I, being fifteen years her senior, was rather embarrassed that I could not keep up with a twenty-eight year old and made some excuse about the chain drive being faulty. She offered to exchange bicycles, but I declined the offer. I arrived at the pub eventually, totally exhausted and out of breath and had not fully recovered after a couple of drinks when it was time to return home. Somehow I managed to make it back whilst complaining bitterly that Joe's bike had something drastically wrong with it! It took several days for my aching muscles to recover. Joe and Peter had a good laugh when I told them about it and it was only then I found out that Helena was super fit, swimming several lengths of the local swimming pool early each morning, before cycling several miles to her work as a lecturer at CWR in Waverley Abbey, near Farnham, Surrey.

Chapter 11

The Lord Heals me – Then my Mother!

by Malcolm

One morning in Autumn 1991, I awoke at around 5.15 am with the most excruciating pain in my left groin and lower left back. I immediately recognised these symptoms as identical to those I had experienced six years previously, when I was diagnosed as having a kidney stone. Six years ago the symptoms had eventually subsided as the stone passed through my body. But the pain had been severe and I had been prescribed the powerful painkiller, 'Temgesic' for the worst bouts of agony. This time I had no painkillers and there were no pharmacies open at that time of the day. I staggered into the bathroom next to my bedroom. As I stood there passing water in agony, my urine turned pink with blood, then a dark ruby red. I was in so much pain, I was beside myself.

I put on my dressing gown and went downstairs. I filled two hot water bottles with boiling water from the kettle and strapped them to my body with the belt of my dressing gown, one on my back and one on my groin. Then I paced the floor of the sitting room alternately groaning and praying in tongues. This went on for several hours. At about 7.15 am, Joe, the owner of the house appeared for breakfast on his way to work. He asked what was the matter with me and I briefly explained the problem through gritted teeth. I said that I would hang on until the doctor's surgery opened later, but that I would be OK. An hour later I was desperate. I had turned on the TV to try and distract my attention from the pain, but to no avail. I was at the absolute end of my tether. Three hours of sheer unremitting, unrelenting agony had worn me out. My strength had drained away and I had entered a strange kind of semi-conscious state where everything seemed unreal and distant. Where was God? How could He let me go through this hell?

About this time, I was right in the middle of our Pastor Derek Brown's nine-week course on healing the sick. I had attended five sessions already. I knew exactly what to do. I declared any unconfessed sin in my life. I pleaded the blood of the Lamb. I bound the works of the enemy and loosed the Holy Spirit. I prayed in tongues. Like Job, I prayed for my friends. I laid hands on myself and commanded healing in my body. Nothing worked!

I waved my fist in the air and shouted at God that if He didn't heal me and take this pain away, I was going to die and I couldn't care less! If that was what He wanted, it was OK by me! I reasoned that if I died I would be with the Lord. If I was healed and allowed to live then that would be OK too. Either way, I would overcome Satan and win. I threw myself on the settee and told the Lord to do whatever He liked and that I had lost interest in the whole damn business.

Suddenly the power of the Spirit fell on me. A current of strong power flowed through my entire body. It felt like warm golden rain which cascaded from the crown of my head to the soles of my feet. The pain in my body which had only moments before been utterly unbearable just melted away and I fell into a deep sleep. Two hours later I awoke feeling refreshed and peaceful. The pain had disappeared and when I went to the bathroom, my urine was normal. I had been completely healed.

That was six years ago and I have had no re-occurrence or further trouble since. I experienced the wonderful grace of God. I learned for myself, that it is only when we come to the end of our own strength, our own resources, our own will-power, that we can begin to draw on His strength, His resources and His power. Often that is exactly the place where God wants us to be totally yielded to Him, totally submitted to Him, totally dependent upon Him. It has made a tremendous difference to my attitude to pain and sickness in my body and in the bodies of others. I now expect without question, that when as a believer, I lay hands on either myself or another who is sick or in pain, that God will act and that person will be healed or at least their condition improved in some way. I have never been disappointed.

However the Lord is the final arbiter in all things and it is His sovereign will that will be done. Our attitude to the will and ability of God to heal us is a personal thing. Everyone has a different pain threshold and no one should be condemned because they turn to a doctor for healing when prayer doesn't seem to work. God uses many ways to heal people and modern conventional medicine is one of them.

Jesus Heals my Mother.

Several months later, I travelled down to Bristol to visit my family unannounced. I arrived at my parent's modest semi-detached house in Downend, a pleasant leafy suburb of Bristol, around lunchtime. I was met at the gate by my ashen-faced father who told me that my mother had been ill all weekend and that the doctor had been sent for. He was obviously very concerned and I asked him what was wrong with her. He described how she had been falling down, suffering black-outs, sickness, pain in the head and she was now virtually blind. My brother had visited earlier that day and apparently was in a real state of distress. Everyone feared the worst. I entered their sitting room where my mother still in her dressing gown, was slumped in an armchair groaning pitifully. My father went into the kitchen to make me a cup of tea. I gently asked my mother how she was. She just groaned some more. The television in the corner was on and the lunchtime news had just started.

It seemed a rather incongruous situation to me. My poor mother, to all intents and purposes, breathing her last, sitting as usual in front of the ubiquitous 'telly'. I sat down on a chair next to my mother and looked at her. She looked pretty bad, her skin a waxy yellow colour, her breathing shallow and erratic. All my life I had never been close to my mother for the reasons I have explained earlier, but at that moment I felt a tremendous sense of pity and deep compassion for her. She looked so frail and pitiful, so lost and defenceless. I didn't know what to do. I didn't know how to pray. I felt totally helpless. I reached out with my left hand and held her right hand which was hanging over the arm of her chair. Suddenly a current of power so strong, that had I not been sitting down would have knocked me off my feet, surged through my entire body. Indescribable power, from the tips of my toes to the top of my head, raced through my body down my left arm, and flowed into my mother's body. Immediately her vision cleared.

'I can see,' she whispered, 'the dizziness and sickness are going, are you a faith healer?' she asked.

'No,' I replied, 'It's not me. This is the power of the Lord Jesus, who is working in you. It's He who is healing you.'

The power continued to flow. I just sat there like some fuse in a circuit and held on. I was reminded of those hand-cranked electrical current generators we had in our school science classroom. You held one contact whilst cranking a handle and experiencing a mild electric shock. The challenge amongst the kids was to see how much power you could take until you simply just had to let go because the current had become too strong. After ten minutes of this she had visibly recovered. Her skin colour and breathing were normal, and she could see clearly. My father had returned with my tea which I sipped from the mug I held in one hand, whilst still holding my mother's hand with the other. My father sat down with his drink and we all sat there watching BBC's 'News at One'.

Nobody spoke. After about twenty minutes, my left hand and arm were extremely painful so I let go of my mother's hand. Immediately the flow of power ceased, as though someone had thrown the off switch. My mother had almost completely recovered now and was sitting up cheerfully eating a sandwich and drinking tea. My father wept a bit and said I was a marvel. I said I was not anything of the sort. Gradually my mother's condition began to deteriorate again and her symptoms began to return. She began to be afraid. I was confident though. I knew the Lord was doing something wonderful here.

'You had better have some more,' I said.

I held her hand once more and the same series of events took place. A tremendous surge of what I can only describe as a powerful electric current swept through my body and into hers. The experience for me bordered on being extremely painful, but amazingly, my mother felt nothing. I held her hand during the rest of the TV programme whilst we sat and watched the events of the day's news unfolding in front of us, while the Lord healed my mother.

After twenty minutes of this further treatment, the power in my body subsided, and left as suddenly as it had arrived. My arms and legs ached for days afterwards. My mother was totally healed though. She never experienced any of those symptoms again. When the doctor finally arrived, he examined her and took a blood sample. He confided to me on the way back to his car that he thought that my mother had suffered a brain haemorrhage from which she seemed to have recovered and that at her age she was lucky to be alive. He warned me that in most cases of people of her age, it was likely to occur again and that the outcome could be expected to prove fatal.

That was six years ago, she has had no further problems since and has just returned from a six-week visit to my sister in Perth, Western Australia, travelling on her own all the way there and back. A total of forty-two hours of flying – at the age of seventy nine. That was my first real experience of being used by God to heal someone. There were no great prayers or promises of repentance. No seeking the Lord and pleading with Him to show mercy. It wasn't what I expected at all. I just laid hands on her and she recovered, just like it says in His handbook.

> *'And these signs shall follow those who believe: they will lay hands on the sick and they will recover.'* (Mark 16:17)

I believe in the literal truth of the Bible. God **did** make the heavens and the earth in six of His days. He **did** create man from the dust of the earth and woman from one of his ribs.

Darwin's great evolution myth is simply a theory, and it takes more effort to believe than does God's word! God caused a great cataclysmic flood to destroy all life on earth except Noah and his family and the animals in the Ark. He sent his only begotten Son, Jesus, to destroy the works of Satan and rescue those of mankind who would believe. People are funny though, and my mother has still not made a public commitment of faith in the Lord Jesus Christ. After a few days she had explained away what had happened to her that day and thinks that she probably wasn't as ill as people had thought and that it had probably, 'cleared up, on its own.' But I knew different. I knew what the Lord had done. I learnt that God is sovereign. I knew that great power for healing was released that day. He chooses when He will heal sickness and how and whom He will use to achieve His purposes.

There is no one 'formula' for healing. Jesus healed all who came to Him, but in Nazareth He could perform few miracles because of their unbelief. Some people are not healed even though they may be believers. Some unbelievers are totally healed. It is a futile exercise to try and work out the whys and wherefores of it. It is a mystery. But God knows the hearts of men. He has a plan for all our lives. Our part is to trust Him regardless. When believers lay hands on a sick person in faith we are to exercise the authority we have in Jesus and leave the rest to Him! Divine healing, though a potent demonstration of God's power, is not the most important thing in people's lives. It is only a temporary fix. The human body in this fallen world will eventually wear out and die anyway. Even perfectly healthy people can die suddenly or be killed in an accident, without warning. Ultimate healing, that perfect everlasting health, purchased by His death on the cross, will only be experienced in the glorified body that all believers in the Lord Jesus Christ will receive at His Second Coming.

Salvation, then, is the most important goal in this life.

There is nothing as important on earth, than the wondrous salvation that the shed blood of the Son of God has made possible for all mankind, if they will only believe on Him. I believe that unforgiveness is the major cause of ill health amongst believers and their seeming inability to be healed.

Paul warns us in 1 Corinthians 11:27–32:

> *'Therefore whoever eats this bread or drinks this cup of the Lord in an unworthy manner will be guilty of the body and blood of the Lord. But let a man examine himself, and so let him eat of that bread and drink of that cup. For he who eats and drinks in an unworthy manner eats and drinks judgement to himself, not discerning the Lord's body. For this reason many are weak and sick among you, and many sleep. For if we would judge ourselves, we would not be judged. But when we are judged, we are chastened by the Lord, that we may not be condemned with the world.'*

Moving On

In the summer of 1992, Joe had decided to get married to Val, a very nice young Christian widow with two children. Peter and I had to find somewhere else to live. The house at Church Crookham, near Fleet, seemed to be just what we were looking for. It was a new four-bedroomed detached house with a study and a large double garage. Both Peter and I were divorced, each with two young daughters and it was ideal for their monthly access visits. The study would serve as an office and the garage would store our cleaning equipment and chemicals of the trade. On looking over the property, I jokingly remarked that it would be no good for us as there was no dishwasher, although there was plumbing and a space for one in the kitchen. I joked that if we were meant to live there, God would have to provide us with a dishwasher as well as the £2,000.00 cash that the agent required by way of deposit and advance rental. Peter just looked at me and blinked. We went through our finances and discovered that there was **no way** that we could afford this place. Although we could just about scrape up the monthly rental and outgoings, we just did not have the money that we needed for the deposit. We prayed about it, in the power of agreement and asked the Lord to provide for our needs.

Later that evening the phone rang and an acquaintance of Peter's, Paddy Earp, asked whether we could clean a large apartment belonging to an Arab business client of his, fairly urgently, if possible – next day. The following morning saw Peter and myself unloading our equipment outside the apartment block in Basle Street near Harrods, Knightsbridge, London. We were to clean the whole apartment including all the expensive carpets, curtains and furniture. As we were cleaning the kitchen, Paddy pointed to an AEG dishwasher and said, 'Sheik Almana is going to replace this machine. It's about four years old, and as he's only in England about twice a year, it's almost brand new. You might as well have it if you can find a use for it!'

At the end of the day we loaded the dishwasher into Peter's car and tucked Paddy's cheque for our work into the Bank paying-in book. The final invoice came to just over £2,000.00! In less than twenty-four hours after asking the Lord to provide, our petition had been answered.

Chapter 12

My First Encounter with Israel
by Malcolm

One week-end in July 1992, my friend Nick Kannen-meyer phoned me from Tel-Aviv, Israel.

'I believe the Lord wants you to come out and see Israel,' said Nick.

'Oh really,' I said, without much enthusiasm. 'When?'

'Now,' replied Nick. 'You can stay with me in my tent.'

'My days of roughing it in a tent are over,' I laughed. 'If the Lord wants me out there then He'll have to provide proper accommodation!'

The conversation continued with Nick telling me about his job with a computer company in Tel Aviv and how much he was enjoying Israel. I thought no more about it until two days later, when the phone rang late at night. It was Nick.

'Guess what!' he said excitedly. 'A friend of mine has asked me to look after his luxury apartment for three weeks whilst he and his family are on holiday in Galilee, and I can have who I like to stay with me! God has provided the proper accommodation, so now you can come out!'

I was amazed. I hadn't really thought about a holiday at this time. The carpet cleaning business was taking off and I really didn't think I could spare the time or the money.

'I can't afford it right now,' I said, 'God will have to provide the money as well.'

Nick and I talked provisionally about the arrangements and I said I would let him know, but that I honestly didn't have the money. However, next day a completely unexpected large cleaning job came in, which had to be done right away and my earnings from that would be enough to finance the trip to Israel! I prayed about it and felt right about going, so I phoned Nick back and told him I would be coming out the following week.

I had asked two single Christian lady friends of mine to Sunday lunch and I discussed it with them. Margaret (later to become my wife) was a new friend. She was very attractive, rather quiet and seemed rather aloof. Mina on the other hand was much more my type. Attractive, noisy, exuberant, a real 'life and soul of the party type'. As soon as I mentioned I was going to Israel, Mina said, 'I'll come too!'

I had known Mina for a couple of years, we had gone out together very briefly but that hadn't worked out. I wasn't sure. But she was fired up with enthusiasm and Margaret thought it was a good idea. Mina was a single parent and couldn't afford much, but a friend of hers, Meredith Carter, made a gift to her of the money she needed to come out for one week. I checked with our pastor, Derek Brown, if he thought this arrangement was OK and he said he, 'didn't have a problem with it.'

Mina and I flew out from Gatwick Airport, England, on the first Sunday in August 1992, bound for Ben Gurion Airport, Tel Aviv. I am not the greatest flyer in the world and when I saw all the Hasidic Jews in their black suits, prayer shawls and Homberg hats in the departure lounge nodding their heads and reading aloud from the Torah, I felt like joining them! Somehow though I felt that they might not appreciate my praying in tongues, even though my tongue is Hebrew! The flight, on an A300 Airbus, was pleasant and uneventful and as the plane touched down gently in Israel at 9 pm that evening, the sound of spontaneous applause could be heard throughout the aircraft.

Nick was there at the Airport to greet us, after we cleared security and customs. The thing that struck me first was the noise and the bustle and the heat. People in the street around the Airport Terminal were shouting, pushing and shoving, street traders were selling food, drinks and cheap souvenirs. Arab traders were arguing and haggling with tourists over the price of their merchandise. It seemed like pandemonium.

Nick drove us to Beit Emmanuel, the Christian Hostel, in Jaffa where Mina would be staying. After dropping her off there, he drove to Holon, a suburb of Tel Aviv a few miles away, to his friend's apartment where I would be staying. After sharing a few things with each other and showing me around the extremely well equipped apartment we retired to our bedrooms. My room overlooked the street and was hot and a bit stuffy.

I was determined not to be plagued by mosquitoes which Nick had said could be a nuisance, so I had come prepared with no less than **three** major lines of defence.

1. An electrical gadget which plugged into a wall socket, containing a special tablet that gave off a vapour deadly to mozzies.
2. A pen which was placed in one's top pocket and when twisted gave out a very high pitched signal which was supposed to be similar to the noise a mosquito makes when in distress.
3. An aerosol spray which was sprayed on any areas of one's skin likely to be exposed and thereby attractive to the mosquito.

I think my dear old dad must have influenced me with his tales of his time in North Africa during the war when he was attached to the American 1st Army under General Eisenhower. He wrote a poem at that time about the dreaded mosquito and the equally dreaded yellow Mepacrin tablets issued to the troops:

'Get on parade for your Mepacrin
Fill your tins, jugs, mugs with water,
for tonight is a night of great danger,
not from the son, but the daughter.

Get your net laid out by 20.30 Hours,
in your long pants, yourself array,
for tonight is a night of great danger,
the mosquito is on the way.

A dangerous enemy of mankind,
the blood runs cold and thin,
But I shudder with fright,
and I can't stand the sight,
of that yellow peril called Mepacrin!'

(Charles George Wilson)

So with all my anti-mosquito defences in order, I climbed into bed and eventually fell asleep. At around three o' clock in the morning I woke up and realized I was being bitten!

I swore as I jumped out of bed and switched on the light.

There was no sign of any mosquitos, I listened for their distinctive buzzing sound. Silence. I peered at the walls and ceiling. Nothing. I pulled back the bedclothes and there they were! An army of tiny red ants! In perfect formation, marching up the bed to make a meal of me! I had every protection conceivable against mosquitos, but nothing for **ants**! I was up half the night clobbering them with a shoe and brushing them off the sheets.

But they were undeterred, onwards, onwards they marched!

Next morning Nick had to go to work, so after we ate a typical Israeli breakfast consisting of cereal, eggs, toast coffee, and chilled mango juice, he dropped me off at Beit Emmanuel, near Jaffa to meet Mina. We walked down the narrow streets towards Tel Aviv and spent the day on the nearby beach. The weather was glorious the temperature in the low nineties. The beach was almost deserted. The sea was like a warm bath. At about one o'clock, we lunched at the beach restaurant and discovered the delights of Humus with Pitta bread, Arabic salad and french fries.

The Still Small Voice

At about 5 pm we started back to Beit Emmanuel to meet Nick for dinner. I remembered that I needed to get some ant powder on the way. We passed a few shops, selling mirrors, bathroom fittings, plumbing supplies etc. But none of the shops we passed looked like the type that would sell ant powder. I was about to despair of ever getting any ant powder when I heard a still small voice within me say, 'Try this one – they sell it in there, Malcolm.'

Mina and I walked into a small shop packed out with electrical supplies, cables wires, plugs, meters, hair driers, irons, etc., but no sign of ant powder. Two men stood behind the counter.

'Have you got any ant powder?' I enquired.

One man was talking into a telephone. The other looked at me as if I was mad.

I asked again. They looked at each other and spoke in Hebrew.

'Do you speak English?' I asked.

They shook their heads and said something in Hebrew.

'Come on,' said Mina walking out of the shop, 'You're wasting your time here, Malcolm. No way does this place sell ant powder!'

I was about to follow her out when the small still voice spoke again.

'Stay where you are Malcolm, they **do** sell it here.'

I turned back to the two men, the older one was now off the phone.

'Ant powder,' I said in a loud voice and gesticulated to them scratching my arms and body, and finally wiggling my two index fingers out from my like two antenna. They both burst out laughing and one of them reached under the counter and pulled out a plastic bottle with some Hebrew words and a picture of an ant on the label. I paid for the ant powder, they wrapped the bottle in a brown bag and I ran after Mina.

'Look what I've got,' I cried, 'Ant powder!'

'I don't believe it,' exclaimed Mina. 'That's amazing!'

'No', I said. 'That's God!'

A Lesson in Trusting God

A few days later, Nick and I got up, had breakfast and went down to his car as usual, so he could drop me off at the beach and continue on to his office. Unfortunately, the offside front tyre on Nick's little Peugot 205 was flat as a pancake!

'Oh my God,' Nick cried, 'What am I going to do? I'm going to be late and my boss will go mad!'

'Don't worry Nick,' I said calmly, 'Let me have your jack and wheel brace (USA: lug wrench), and I'll change the wheel.'

Nick looked embarrassed and worried, 'I haven't got a wheel brace.'

'Of course you have,' I said, 'You drove this car out from England, you must have a wheel brace.'

'I think I lost it,' replied Nick, now looking quite nervous.

'What?' I said, 'You drove across Europe with no wheel brace?'

'Well, I didn't think I would need one,' he spluttered. 'Besides, I drove into the Sinai Desert as well – and I didn't have any trouble then!'

After I told him what I thought of him, we began to ask passing motorists if we could borrow their wheel braces. It soon became obvious that the wheel braces issued with cars in Israel were a completely different size to English ones. We even tried some nearby garages and auto-shops but it was no use. By this time Nick was in a near panic. He returned to the apartment to phone his boss and tell him he would be late. In the meantime waiting by the car, I somehow managed to shut the car door which then automatically locked, with the ignition keys still inside. I went back to the apartment. Nick was on the phone.

'Have you got a spare set of keys?' I asked casually.

'No,' replied Nick. 'What do you want them for?'

I explained to Nick that he shouldn't worry too much about his flat tyre, as now I had locked his keys in his car as well! Nick looked pale. I remembered an old trick I had seen done with a piece of plastic palleting tape, so I managed to find something similar and after a few minutes fiddling about I got the car door open and retrieved the keys. Out on the street I stopped a few more drivers and asked to borrow their wheel braces, but it was no good, they spoke only Hebrew. I didn't know what to do next, so I prayed out loud in tongues, more in frustration than anything else, for I wasn't feeling particularly spiritual at that moment. Just then that still small voice spoke to me.

'You're wasting your time talking to these people Malcolm, they don't understand a word you say! Go and get Nick and start again. Just do everything as if you **really** have a wheel brace, and I'll do the rest!'

My spirit leapt within me. God was going to solve the problem. I had no doubt.

All **we** had to do was – just do as He said! I ran back upstairs.

'Nick, we're going,' I beamed. Nick was still on the phone. He covered the mouthpiece with his hand and looked at me.

'You've had a word!' he exclaimed.

'That's right,' I said. 'Come on we're going.'

We rushed down to the car.

'Get the spare wheel and pass it to me,' I said.

'But you haven't got a wheel brace,' said Nick, incredulously.

'Just do it!' I said, rather firmly.

Nick undid the butterfly nut holding the spare wheel under the rear of the car, whilst I got the jack in place, raised the front of the car, then held my hand out towards Nick to receive from him the wheel brace that we didn't have!

Nick was almost finished undoing the spare wheel. At the very moment Nick freed the spare wheel and as it touched the ground, a car pulled up alongside and a young man got out. He took one look at us, opened up the boot of his car, reached in and handed Nick a combination wheel brace, with about eight different sizes of socket. Nick placed it in my already outstretched hand and I quickly found the right size socket and changed the wheel. I handed the brace back to Nick, he handed it back to the young man, who placed it back in his car and drove off. All this took about two minutes without a word being spoken by any of us. A few minutes later we were on our way.

Nick couldn't stop laughing. 'I don't believe it!' he cried, 'that was amazing, that guy must have been an angel or something.'

Just then I received a word from the Lord.

'Nick,' I said, 'Your Father says to you, that you are to reach out to Him in the **supernatural**, for the things you need in the **natural**.'

A Man of the Spirit

Near the end of Mina's week we were eating our evening meal in the garden at Beit Emmanuel when a middle-aged man wearing a dark suit, a purple shirt and white dog-collar, sat down at our table opposite Mina and me. We began to engage him in conversation. He was an American, Bishop John Stanley, of the Orthodox Church of the East, Vashon, Washington State. He asked if we had been to any of the typical places of religious interest, the Holy Sepulchre, the Garden Tomb, or the Via Della Rosa in Jerusalem. I replied that we were more interested in lazing on the beach and thanking the Lord for His goodness, than going on religious tours. He laughed and said that Jesus was just as likely to be found on the beach with us as in those religious places.

There was something about this man. He smiled knowingly and talked about Jesus as if He were a personal friend. He spoke about things of the Spirit with a knowledge and confidence that I had seen in no man, before or since. At the end of the meal we were still deep in conversation with him when we noticed that the three of us were the only ones left in the garden. John Stanley looked around.

'I guess it must be you two,' he said.

He went on to explain that he should have returned to America the day before, but God had told him to delay his journey by one day and go to the garden at Beit Emmanuel. He was to wait until there were only two people left in the garden with him after the meal. These would be the people God wanted him to speak to.

He reached across the table and lightly held my wrist.

'You are blessed,' was all he said. My eyes immediately filled with tears.

He smiled. He began to talk softly to Mina, holding her hand. The tears rolled down her face. At that moment Nick arrived and led me away across the road to meet a Christian Arab friend of his. When I asked Nick about this later, he said he felt that God told him he should lead me away, so that Mina and John Stanley could talk in private.

Later that evening we arranged to take Bishop Stanley to

the nearby Dan Panorama Hotel where he would catch a coach to the Airport. Nick, Mina and I went back to the hotel and had a coffee with him. He spoke to several people like busboys and waitresses in their native Hebrew. They all reacted in the same way; they went quiet, their eyes filled up and some burst into tears, as he spoke into their lives what must surely have been powerful words of knowledge, straight from the Father's heart. We bade him farewell. We had all been deeply touched by something in this man.

Nick said later, that he might have been an angel.

At the end of my first week in Israel, Mina had to return home. Nick and I drove her to the Airport. We had all had a marvellous time. We had visited the Dead Sea, Ein Geddi Nature Reserve, the beautiful old town of Jaffa, Christ Church Jerusalem and of course Tel Aviv, my favourite city in Israel. The Dead Sea is well named. I have never been to a more inhospitable place in my life. The temperature was 120 degrees in the shade, except there isn't any shade! It is the lowest point on earth below sea-level, so the atmospheric pressure is intense. Every breath of the stifling super-heated air sears the chest and lungs. Nick took us to a 'beach' near the car park. We had to walk across sharp flint-like stones which cut my feet. As soon as we waded into the still, hot water of the sea, my cut feet stung like billy-o. I couldn't wait to get out again. We were in the company of a group of unhappy looking people, mostly Arabs. I asked Nick if this was where the Israelis came to bathe. Nick said it was.

Now if I learned anything on my trip to Israel, I learned that the Israelis know how to do things well and I couldn't believe that they would put up with such discomfort. Later driving a few kilometres further along the sea-shore, we passed a very futuristic, glass domed, Aqua-marina complex, with swimming pools and restaurants and complete air-conditioning. I found out later, that is where the Israelis bathe in the Dead Sea, and where we should have gone!

My second week sped by. We visited the Sea of Galilee, then Jerusalem again, which was hot and humid. We spent most of our time in Tel Aviv. We met a young English Jewish believer called Kay Wilson. She was a talented artist and musician with a great sense of humour who had made Allyia to Israel several years earlier and was now an Israeli citizen. I learned a lot about the Israeli people. How hard working they are, how talented, but how barely tolerant of tourists, especially Christians. They are a stubborn and tough people. They are natural survivors. They have had to be. They have suffered a lot at the hands of the world, particularly from Christians. They are not easy to get on with, but there is something about them that is attractive and mysterious. They are God's chosen people and from the Jews came the Messiah our Saviour. They are the natural branches, temporarily broken off for the sake of us Gentiles. The Lord says:

> *'I will bless those who bless them and curse those who curse them.'*

I choose blessing.

A House Divided

The carpet cleaning business prospered for the rest of the year. We even launched a scheme in which other carpet cleaners could take a franchise using our company name and marketing methods. However at this stage things began to go badly wrong. As we grew in size, the importance of delivering a top quality service to our customers became ever more important. However when some major operational difficulties arose, Peter and I had what could be called 'a difference of opinion'. The writing was on the wall. I sought the Lord on the whole matter and received many words and scriptures indicating that, *'a house divided against itself cannot stand.'*

By April 1993 work dried up and we had only our two original contacts left to supply our income. The franchise idea had run into problems. Peter and I were no longer in agreement about how the business should be run. It is pointless now to go into the details or apportion blame but after several meetings together with our respective pastors, the four of us decided that it would be best if Peter and I went our separate ways. Peter decided that he could no longer afford his share of the rent and somehow managed to convey the impression to the landlord that I could not either. I received notice to quit. I was not very happy. After months of strain and tension in trying to keep the business going, I was now to be out on the street! I could not understand how things had reached this sorry state. How could the Lord who had blessed our business so abundantly have allowed the whole thing to turn so sour? I shouted at Him at the top of my voice, 'Why, Lord – Why?'

I was devastated – hadn't I experienced enough failure in my life?

Just when things seemed to be getting back on an even keel, the ground beneath my feet had turned to quicksand! My pastor, Derek said it was because God could not bless unrighteousness, and that it had crept into our business. The day I received the notice to quit I was having a meal with my friends Joe and Val, now married at their home in Fourmarks, Hants.

I showed them the notice to quit letter and said, 'Where am I going to live now?'

Val said that a friend of hers had a house in Farnborough that had stood empty for a year whilst she tried to sell it and that she might be interested in renting it.

Val gave me the phone number and I viewed the old cottage that week-end. Although it was not ideal, it was cheap and I could still run a small carpet cleaning business from there, using a couple of machines I had managed to retain together with the Toshiba contract, as part of the disposal agreement with Peter.

We agreed the rent and I moved in a few weeks later. God had provided for me yet again!

Chapter 13

My Father Comes to Jesus and Goes Home

by Malcolm

One day in spring 1993 my mother phoned. 'Your father's had a seizure of some sort and they've taken him into hospital,' she said. 'He's been having terrible shaking fits in his sleep during the past few nights.'

I knew my father hadn't been right for some time. He would fall asleep in his chair sometimes and awake with a start not knowing where he was or recognising anyone around him. His memory too had been failing over recent years and he was slowing up quite noticeably. I phoned the hospital where they'd taken him and spoke to the ward sister.

'As far as we can tell,' she informed me, 'your father is suffering from bleeding in the brain. The condition that is causing his problems is called "multi infarct dementure".'

I asked her how serious the condition was and she replied that, 'Although in your father's case it is not immediately life-threatening, it is progressive and he will gradually become worse.' She explained that the brain cells become deprived of blood and die off, leading eventually to death.

I drove down to Bristol that night with Margaret, the Christian lady whom I had known for a year and had been recently 'dating' during the past week or so. We drove straight to the hospital in Margaret's Renault and parked outside in the visitors car park. We sat in the car and prayed. I bound the works of the enemy in that hospital and loosed the power of the Holy Spirit to be with us as we visited my father. Margaret agreed with my prayer and Amen-ed. We both felt the power of the Spirit present in our bodies as we prayed – particularly in our hands and arms. As we entered the secure ward the smell of urine and disinfectant filled our nostrils. A half-dressed elderly man, was shuffling along the corridor, occasionally shouting obscenties through his drooling mouth. Strange groans and cries filled the air, as we walked past rooms with their doors open and observed mainly old men in various stages of what seemed like torment. I sensed the mocking presence of demonic spirits in this place of sickness and death. I prayed softly in tongues, claiming the blood of Jesus over the power of Satan and all his principalities and powers.

My father was sitting at a table in pyjamas and dressing gown in the day room with my brother John. The patients had just been given tea and we got two cups from the servery and sat down with them. I introduced Margaret, whom my family had not met before. I had my New King James Bible under my arm and placed it on the table before me. After exchanging the usual pleasantries, my brother bade us farewell, kissed my father goodbye and got up to go. I accompanied him to the ward door with its combination lock.

I reassured my brother, 'Don't worry about Dad,' I said. 'God's in control.'

My brother who is not yet a believer made no comment. I returned to the day room where Margaret was sitting holding my father's hand. I felt we should get down to business right away.

I opened my Bible and Margaret and I held my father's hands in ours as we softly prayed the Lord's prayer over him. Suddenly on the next table two old men who had been sitting quietly up till then started arguing loudly. One threatened to punch the other and they stood to their feet and squared up to each other fists clenched. I discerned immediately what this was all about and that the enemy was behind it, so I prayed louder. I suggested that we go to my father's room where we could have some peace and quiet. My father sat on his bed smiling like a little child. Although the seizure had affected his mind, at that stage in his illness, he could still understand most things. Margaret and I sat next to him. Although not a church-goer himself, all my life my father had always talked with great reverence about 'the Lord Jesus Christ' and how he believed that He had looked after him in troubled times and also during the war when he had served in the army. I remember it was my father who walked out of the room when I related my experiences of Bill the spirit medium, before I was saved. He muttered then that, 'it wasn't right!' How right he was. I asked him whether he believed in Jesus. After a few moments he nodded and replied, 'Yes!' He seemed surprised that I should be asking the question. I explained that it was necessary to publicly confess Jesus before men and that we should repent of our sins, ask Jesus for forgiveness and receive Him into our hearts. I asked him if he would like to do this and pray the prayer of salvation with us. He replied without hesitation, 'Yes.'

So that night in that little hospital room, my father prayed with us the sinner's prayer and gave his life to the Lord. We laid hands on him and commanded healing to his body and felt the power of the Holy Spirit flow into him. Later that week we visited my father again and met my brother coming out on his way to the car park. My brother was very excited and pleased about the terrific improvement in my father's condition. We continued visiting him during the rest of the year. One particular night Margaret and I laid hands on him and immediately he reacted.

'Ooh,' he said 'Good vibrations!'

I asked him if he knew what it was. 'Yes,' he replied.

'What?' I asked.

'Jesus!' he said.

During all the months up to his death we continued to lay hands on him and pray for his healing. We never once failed to feel the power of the Holy Spirit flowing through us into his body. We believed that he would be healed, although he gradually became worse. On 10th December 1993 I received a phone call from my sister Diane's husband, Renato, saying that my father's condition had deteriorated suddenly and he had been taken to Frenchay Hospital where he was not expected to live through the night. Margaret drove us down the motorway to Bristol at a steady 70 mph. I was worried that we might arrive too late and told her to drive faster.

'No Malcolm,' she said. 'The Lord has told me, nothing is going to happen before we get there.'

We arrived about 10 pm and went straight to the men's ward where my father lay unconscious, surrounded by my family, his bed screened off from the other patients.

I asked the ward sister what had happened. She said that my father's liver and bowels had stopped working and that there was widespread internal bleeding. He was on a morphine drip to ease his pain and he was not expected to live much longer. He was beyond medical help. Margaret and I joined the rest of the family at his bedside. My mother looked tired and worn. My younger sister and sister-in-law were tearful, my brother grim-faced. Margaret and I held my father's thin frail hands and immediately felt the flow of the Holy Spirit's power and we both sensed that although my father was unconscious, he knew that we had arrived. My family had held their bedside vigil for most of the day and I suggested that they should take a break and go and have some coffee. A few minutes later, just Margaret and myself were at my father's bedside.

As I read aloud the 23rd Psalm, the background noise in the ward began to increase. The elderly man in the next bed began to shout. This continued for several minutes. I became angry. My father had a right to die in peace, I told Margaret.

'I bind you Satan and all your works in the mighty name of Jesus,' I said in a loud voice. 'In the name of Jesus Christ of Nazareth, I command you to be still!'

It is difficult to find the words to describe adequately what happened next, but a complete and utter silence fell on that small area of the ward. It was like the eye of a hurricane had moved over my father's bed and at that moment there was perfect peace. I cried out to the Lord to have mercy and end my father's suffering. Margaret and I prayed that He should either heal him or take him. My father's breathing became shallower and shallower. I waited for the sound of his next breath, but it never came.

Then the most wonderful and amazing thing happened. Margaret and I suddenly became aware of an invisible presence enter the area where we were seated around my father's bed and after a minute or so, we felt **two** unseen presences depart.

We both knew that either an angel or the Lord Jesus Himself, had come into our presence and led my father's spirit home.

I looked at my father; his skin was rapidly turning a parchment yellow, the life had gone from him, and all that was left here was an empty container, a shell. I was both sad and elated. For the first time in my life I had seen someone die. Margaret and I shared later that when we witnessed the departure of my father's spirit, we felt not only tremendous joy for him, but that in a strange sort of way we felt very envious. We felt that we had wanted to also go with that angel and leave this world behind. But we soon agreed that no-one goes before their time and that God had work for us to do first. I broke the news to my family as they returned from the rest-room.

We all said our farewells to Charles George Wilson until the hospital staff asked us to leave whilst they examined him. In an adjacent room with the family I started to read aloud a passage from the Book of Revelation:

> 'And I saw a new heaven and a new earth, for the first . . . '

That was as far as I got before I was overcome with tears.
Margaret continued:

> ' . . . for the first heaven and the first earth had passed away. Also there was no more sea. Then I, John, saw the holy city, New Jerusalem, coming down out of heaven from God, prepared as a bride adorned for her husband. And I heard a loud voice from heaven saying, "Behold, the tabernacle of God is with men, and He will dwell with them, and they shall be His people, and God Himself will be with them and be their God. And God will wipe away every tear from their eyes; there shall be no more death, nor sorrow, nor crying; and there shall be no more pain, for the former things have

*passed away." Then He who sat on the Throne said,
"Behold, I make all things new." And He said to me, "Write,
for these words are true and faithful." And He said to me, "It
is done! I am the Alpha and Omega, the Beginning and the
End. I will give of the fountain of the water of life freely to
him who thirsts. He who overcomes shall inherit all things,
and I will be his God and he shall be My son." '*

(Revelation 21:1–7)

My family were deeply touched by these words. My
sister Diane and her husband Renato became believers a
few months later and in July 1994 were baptised at their
local Spirit-filled church, Christ the Rock, at Yate, near
Bristol.

The rest of my family have still to make a decision for the
Lord, but Margaret and I are praying for them and we believe
they will be saved. I learnt a lot from my father's death. I
learnt that God does not always answer prayers the way we
expect Him to. Margaret and I had been praying for my
father's healing. But God was looking to perform a much
greater work. My father was saved into the Kingdom and
through the effect of his death on their lives, also my sister
and her husband came to know the Lord. My brother has
been affected also, although he doesn't know it yet!

On the day before my father died, my brother made his
usual daily visit to the Hospital. For several months my
father had lost his faculty of coherent speech and could not
walk. When my brother went to his room to visit him my
father was nowhere to be seen. My brother eventually found
him walking normally through the ward and speaking
fluently, according to my brother, a strange language which
he thought to be 'French'. My father had never learned
French. I know that he had been filled with the Spirit and
was talking to my brother in tongues! Next day he was taken
home!

I learnt from my father's illness and death that we
should not only look on the outward appearance. That
we should not consider the physical circumstances however
hopeless they might appear to be, but look on the Lord
Jesus. After all, the cross is foolishness to those who are

perishing. The crucifixion was a disgusting filthy business. On the outward a troublemaker, a blasphemer, was scourged almost to death, tortured, abused, stripped naked and nailed to a cross. Imagine the stench of Golgotha, in that hot sun; the bloody mess of entrails and intestines hanging out of a gaping spear wound in the side of a man who had probably lost all control of his bodily functions.

Yet that man Jesus,

> '...who for the joy that was set before Him endured the cross, despising the shame, and has sat down at the right hand of the throne of God.'   (Hebrews 12:2)

It was Satan and all his works that died that day! Jesus nailed them all to the tree. Satan, sin, sickness, death, Hades, rebellious angels, the whole rotten lot.

Judgement was pronounced upon them that day. All that remains is for the sentence to be carried out at His Glorious Second Coming, when all His enemies will be put under His feet! Nowadays, when I look at my father's photograph which sits on my desk, I burst out laughing! That doesn't sound very respectful to the memory of my dead father, now does it?

My father was quite a proud man and to see him senile and doubly incontinent for the last year of his life, was very upsetting for us all, especially my mother. But I know he is not dead – but alive and in perfect health! I know without a shadow of doubt that I shall see him again. I laugh with him, not at him.

I laugh at all the sickness, pain and suffering that the devil tried to bind him with in his last days. But thanks to the Lord Jesus, my father has had the last laugh!

He has through faith and belief in the Lord Jesus Christ, overcome sickness, disease pain and suffering. He has overcome Satan himself and will receive the blessed hope of all believers – eternal life in the presence of the Lord!

If only mankind would stop and consider for just one minute – stop all the fighting and killing – stop all the dishonesty and crime – stop all the sinning and self-destructive behaviour. If only ... If only...

Jesus said when He wept over Jerusalem:

> *'I wanted to gather your children together, as a hen gathers her chicks under her wings but you were not willing!'*

The days of Satan's rule on this planet are shortly coming to an end, praise God. That day will soon come when all of mankind will look upon the one they have pierced and mourn.

> *'Then every knee shall bow and every tongue confess that Jesus Christ is Lord, to the Glory of God the Father.'*

Chapter 14

The Marriage of Malcolm
and Margaret
by Malcolm

Margaret and I were married on my birthday the 28th May 1994. I was forty-seven years old and Margaret two years older. I had been married twice before and Margaret once. None of our marriages had been Christian marriages, so this time it was different. We knew the Lord had brought us together for His purposes as well as to bless us. We were married at the King's Church, Aldershot, England by our pastor, Derek Brown. We had completed a six-month marriage preparation course run by the church so we had not entered into this commitment lightly. Margaret's father Jack a retired Reverend, gave her away and she looked radiant, just as a bride should on her wedding day. Many friends and relations came from as far away as Australia and the USA and we were extremely blessed by the generosity of everyone concerned. Margaret serenaded me with a beautiful song which she had co-written with a friend of ours, Justin Frost who accompanied her on acoustic guitar. Justin is a very talented Christian musician and songwriter, so the result of their efforts was simply wonderful.

'I'll Always Be Here For You'

'This song is just for you, a simple way to say I do,
So much of love is unspoken,

We have so much to share, so many ways to show we
    care,
Who set this new love in motion,
And I know that this love is for eternity,
Safe in the Father's hands,
Full of His grace, full of His truth,
United and able to stand,

And I'll always, always, always be here for you,
I'll always, always, always be here for you,

And so I give to you all I am to start anew
This is a day we'll remember,
And now that we are one and this adventure has
    begun,
We'll share the future together,
And I know that this love is for eternity,
Safe in the Father's hands,
Full of His joy, full of His truth,
United and able to stand,

And I'll always, always always be here for you,
I'll always, always, always be here for you,

And I know that this love is for eternity,
Safe in the Fathers hands,
Full of His grace, full of His truth,
United and able to stand,

And I'll always, always, always be here for you,
I'll always, always, always be here for you.'
(Words: Justin Frost and Margaret Wilson
Music: Justin Frost)

We had arranged to honeymoon in Israel, a country that
Margaret had always longed to visit and that I had visited
two years before. Our air tickets and hotel reservation details
had somehow failed to arrive in the post as promised by the
travel company; I was not very pleased. However, Margaret
spoke to the agent by telephone who told us just to turn up
at the airport, give our names at the checkout and assured us
that everything would be alright. We did just that and some

four-and-a-half hours later we landed at Tel Aviv airport.
After travelling from the airport by taxi we checked in at the
five-star Dan Panorama Hotel situated on the sea front, at
the Jaffa end of Tel Aviv's magnificent golden beach.

Next day we walked along the esplanade in the brilliant
sunshine to the beautiful medieval town of Jaffa, with its
narrow streets and winding passages full of little shops, art
galleries and craft workshops. I had been unsure of going to
Israel for our honeymoon at all, finances being rather
limited but I had prayed about the trip and sought the Lord
on whether we should make the trip or not.

I had 'received' a passage of scripture from 2 Chronicles
2:16 which seemed to confirm that we should go:

> 'And we will cut wood from Lebanon, as much as you need:
> we will bring it to you in rafts by sea to Joppa (Jaffa), and
> you will carry it up to Jerusalem.'

The first place we visited in Jaffa was an architectural
excavation/exhibition under the central square in Jaffa.
Right in the entrance was a large illuminated cabinet
displaying the following passage of scripture in both Hebrew
and English:

> 'And it came to pass in the days of King Solomon ... "And
> we will cut wood out of Lebanon, as much as thou shalt
> need ... " etc.'

It was exactly the same passage of scripture, which the
Spirit had 'quickened' to me, only a few days before!
Confirmation indeed.

The Dan Panorama Hotel was extremely comfortable and
the service typically Israeli. On the Saturday of the first week
I was intrigued to read on the entertainments notice board,

> 'A Demonstration of Telepathic and Psychic
> Powers will be given in the first floor lounge
> at 10 am.'

Margaret and I had noticed that the Synagogue in the
basement of the hotel was deserted. We had hoped to sit at

the back and perhaps join in some praise and worship, but after waiting some time no-one turned up. We made our way to the first floor lounge which by ten minutes past ten contained a sizeable audience for the show. A large Israeli man in his thirties had the audience 'spellbound' with his apparently, amazing psychic feats. We sat at the back for a few minutes and prayed quietly in tongues against this deceptive display of occult power.

We discovered later that this type of show was to be seen every Saturday in all the Dan Hotels in the Tel Aviv area, as part of their entertainments programme. We complained to the General Manager and told him of our disappointment that this type of thing should be going on in Israel and especially on the Shabbat. We told him that it was quite ludicrous that the hotel had special Shabbat elevators which stopped at every floor, whilst occult shows were taking place in his lounge. (It is a rule for religious Jews that they must not operate any electrical equipment on the Shabbat.) I regret to relate that our complaints fell on deaf ears.

Israel, I'm afraid, is a country of tremendous contrast and the centre of every kind of spiritual aberration one can think of. There are even two guys walking about Jerusalem in white sheets, purporting to be the two witnesses mentioned in the Book of Revelation. Margaret and I discovered some time later that throughout the Bible, the tribe of Dan, was always mixed up in idol worship and things detestable to God. We later learned that in the Book of Revelation, the tribe of Dan are the only tribe out of the twelve tribes of Israel who are not sealed by God (Revelation 7:7). Their place is taken by the Levites, who were of course not a tribe, but separated unto God as the priesthood.

As we had arrived in Israel with no air tickets, we had none for the return flight to England. At the beginning of our second week I telephoned the local travel representative and enquired as to how we would get home.

'Come along to the office, and I'll issue your return tickets,' said the woman on the phone.

After receiving directions on how to find her office, I thought that they were rather complicated and requested that she had the tickets delivered to our hotel, because after all, her company had failed to get the originals to us.

'If you want to go home, **you** come round here,' she replied in typical Israeli fashion. 'Otherwise – Israel is a nice place to live, you'll enjoy it!' she said replacing her receiver.

A few days later we decided to walk to the travel agent's office just off Ben Yehuda Street in the commercial centre of Tel Aviv. As usual the sun was hot at around 11 am so we strolled along in no particular hurry. Suddenly there was the sound of screeching brakes and the squealing of tyres. There was a loud bang. I looked across the wide street just in time to see a young woman thrown high up in the air like some rag doll, land on a car's windscreen, smashing it in pieces with her head, and continue bouncing along the car's roof, landing with a sickening thump in the road behind.

The driver got out of the car and tore his clothes. He screamed in Hebrew at the girl and started shouting at the gathering crowd. The traffic came to a standstill behind and immediately everyone sounded their horns and shouted. The driver examined his car and seemed to be complaining to the small crowd gathering on the busy pavement about the damage his vehicle had sustained. Nobody went to her.

The young girl was lying in a heap on the ground. Still nobody went to her.

I ran across to her and cradled her head in my arms and she sat up, moaning quietly. Her face was badly cut up and blood was streaming from a deep head wound. She was still conscious but in a state of shock. I didn't know what to do so I prayed in tongues. She moaned something in English about not wanting to go to hospital. I said that she would have to go to hospital but that she would be all right, Jesus would look after her.

I felt power flowing down my arms through my hands and into her body. The traffic continued to pile up behind us, with drivers shouting angrily and waving their fists in the air. I shouted at a bystander to call an ambulance and Margaret came over to us. After ten minutes still no-one had come near. The driver was now explaining the situation to two policemen who had arrived and were re-directing the traffic. The bleeding stopped and eventually a woman came out of a nearby shop and offered to let the girl sit in her premises until the ambulance arrived.

Margaret whispered to me that she had said to the Lord, 'Lord that girl must be in a bad way!'

Immediately the Lord had replied, 'No, she is OK!'

After nearly **half an hour** an Ambulance arrived with the sign 'American Hospital' on its side. The para-medics led the young woman clutching a towel to her head, into the ambulance. She actually walked into the ambulance under her own 'steam' and sat down as it sped off. Car drivers in Tel Aviv drive extremely fast and vehicles double park on both sides of the road. Pedestrians are prone to just step out into the street without warning and that is what happened on this occasion. I have seen a few serious accidents in my time and some badly injured people. There was no way in the natural, that she could have sustained injuries like those and 'walked' onto an ambulance.

Margaret and I believe that the Lord ministered healing to her that day and that somehow we were meant to be in that particular street. On that particular day, the Kingdom of God came near to that young woman.

The passing motorists and the bystanders seemed to be disinterested in the poor girl's plight. I'm sure that this was not really the case, but there has been so much bloodshed in Israel that the people who live there must have become rather hardened to such scenes.

Chapter 15

My First Trip to America
by Malcolm

Near the end of August 1995, Margaret, my daughters Adrienne, Winona and I arrived at the Dollar Car Rental Desk at Orlando Airport at about 5 pm ET. Margaret handed the rental clerk our booking details for the Dodge Spirit car which we had booked in England, when I had jokingly said to her, 'I ain't drivin no dodgey spirit!'

The clerk typed the information into her computer terminal.

'I'm just gonna upgrade your car three levels to a Chrysler New Yorker,' she said. 'It's a lovely car.'

'Thank you,' we said, not knowing what a Chrysler New Yorker was.

'Can I have your credit card?' she asked.

'We don't have any,' we replied.

'Oh dear,' she said. 'We can't rent you a car without a credit card. Well anyway, where are you staying?' she asked.

Margaret answered, 'With my sister, in Myrtle Beach, South Carolina.'

'Oh dear,' said the clerk. 'You can't take our cars across the State line!'

I said, 'But we hired this car in the UK and nobody mentioned anything about not being allowed to take it out of Florida!'

'Where are you staying tonight, sir?' the clerk asked.

'We thought we would find a motel somewhere,' I said.

'Which one?' she asked.

Margaret replied, 'You think of a name, you know the area.'

'OK,' she said. 'I'll put you down as staying at, let's see, hmmm … The Quality Inn, that's as good as any.'

The clerk seemed to have ignored the fact that we had no credit cards, intended to drive the car out of the State, and what's more she never even asked us for the large cash deposit we had expected to pay. We signed the paperwork, she checked our driving licences and passports and gave us a slip of paper to release the car to us. We made our way to the car storage area and were directed to this big beautiful brand new, gleaming white car. Now I have owned Audis, Volvos, BMWs etc., but this car was the best I had ever driven. It was luxury with a capital L. Air conditioned, automatic, quiet, smooth, electric everything.

Some of our American friends told us later, 'It's impossible to even rent a five dollar video movie for the night without a credit card, and you didn't even have to leave a cash deposit! You've got a brand new, thirty-five thousand dollar car there – it's impossible – just impossible!'

They were astounded, but we knew it was God's wonderful provision. With God nothing is impossible. Why He had even arranged for a top of the range rental car for us! To me it was further confirmation that God can provide abundantly for His people regardless of the rules and regulations of man. I believe that He will provide for His people during the Great Tribulation, even when all buying and selling transactions can only be made by having the mark of the beast. God's people who have faith in Him and refuse to take the mark, will not go hungry or have no roof over their heads. Remember the Children of Israel who wandered in the desert for forty years? They were provided with their daily bread, they had shade from the sun during the day and fire for warmth by night. Even their clothes and shoes never wore out during all that time.

I drove out of the airport terminal and as we headed towards what we thought was the route to Orlando, Margaret navigated. Now Margaret does not have the greatest sense of direction in the world and we were soon lost. I saw a sign for Kissamee.

'Let's find a motel,' I said, tired and a little bit irritable.

We pulled into the driveway of the first motel we came to and guess what?

The sign above read, '**Quality Inn**'!

I felt that we were to share the exiting things the Lord had shown to us about the Rapture and the Second coming of the Lord, with Charles and Frances Hunter, the famous American Evangelists and Healers. I felt that in some way yet to be revealed, they were to be important in relation to the insight and understanding that the Lord had given Margaret and me. We had met them a few months previously in Manchester, England, where they had been ministering at the Bethshan Tabernacle Church. We had spent four days with them in Manchester, learning about their methods of healing the sick by the power of the Spirit, and also learning of the wonderful way the Lord is using them to spread the Gospel of Jesus Christ worldwide, especially in Russia. They made a huge impression on Margaret and myself with their infectious enthusiasm for the things of God and the way they have been blessed with an exceptional ability to minister in the power of the Spirit. They are mightily used by God in their miracle healing ministry and powerful evangelism and are only too willing to impart to others what they have learned over the years.

We sent a fax to their office in Houston, Texas telling them when we proposed to be in the States and asked if we could see them and share what we had. We explained that the nearest we would be to Houston would be South Carolina and that we would be taking the kids down to Disneyland during our stay. In the meantime we obtained details of flights to Myrtle Beach SC and discovered that the only flights left were via Fort Worth, Dallas, Texas. We decided that if the Hunters would see us, we would stop over en route and travel from Dallas to Houston. But before we had received a reply to our fax and could reserve our tickets to Myrtle Beach, I felt the Lord direct us not to fly via Dallas but rather fly direct to Orlando in Florida and that we should hire a car at the airport then drive to Myrtle Beach. Margaret agreed that this felt right and she felt also that the Hunters might even be in Florida for some reason, perhaps on holiday. We checked the airlines and only Virgin Atlantic had a direct flight to Orlando on the date we wanted to travel with four seats left! We duly booked those seats. That evening a fax arrived from the Hunters saying that they would be pleased to meet us. They enclosed details of their schedule showing that whilst we were in the USA they were due to be ministering in the Carpenters Home Church in Lakeland Florida, some forty miles from where we were to be in Orlando! The Carpenters Home Church of course is where Rodney Howard Brown is well known as the man who brought the latest move of God's Spirit which came later to be known incorrectly as the Toronto Blessing. We sincerely believe that God had directed our steps so that we would meet up with them at exactly the right time and place so that His purposes should be fulfilled.

We arrived at Margaret's sister Jane's house in Myrtle Beach after a long drive from Florida on the Interstate highway. Later that evening we shared with Jane what we felt the Lord had shown us regarding the rapture of the church and the second coming and in particular the scripture from 2 Peter 3:8:

> *'But, beloved, do not forget this one thing, that with the Lord one day is as a thousand years, and a thousand years as one day.'*

Jane later suggested that we spend the week-end in Charlotte where her daughters and granddaughter could meet us and we could have a family time together. This would mean that we would miss the Sunday morning service in Jane's church, the Coastal Christian Centre in Myrtle Beach. I felt that the Lord specifically wanted us to visit Jane's church on Sunday and we therefore declined the invitation to make the trip to Charlotte. We were astonished then, when Leon Webber, the Pastor of Jane's church began his Sunday morning word with the scripture from 2 Peter 3:8:

> *'But, beloved, do not forget this one thing, that with the Lord one day is as a thousand years, and a thousand years as one day.'*

The whole of his following teaching was on the subject of the rapture of the body of Christ and the tribulation. Jane, in particular, was amazed and she passed us a note saying that he had never spoken on this scripture before! At the end of his message we went up to him, shook his hand and thanked him. I explained to him that I somehow felt it was the Lord's will that we should be there that morning and that when we heard his opening scripture, we knew it was right for us to be there. I gave him a copy of a synopsis of what we believe the Lord had shown us regarding the rapture and the second coming and later that day after lunch, we left the beautiful resort of Myrtle Beach and travelled back to Orlando.

Towards the end of our stay in the States, we drove from Orlando to Lakeland to meet with Charles and Frances Hunter in the Carpenters Home Church. We had arranged a brief meeting with Charles in order that we might share with them. Charles showed us into a small conference room and introduced us to their long-time friend and associate, Mr Russell Bixler, Chairman and CEO of Cornerstone Christian TV network based in Pittsburgh, PA.

Before we began to share with them, Russell began by asking us, 'Is what you have unique?'

Margaret and I looked at each other and answered, 'Yes, we believe it is.'

We shared with Charles and Russell for about half an hour and at the end of this time Russell agreed that what we had was indeed unique and that he had not come across it before. Russell suggested a short time of prayer and during that time he prayed that the Lord would give us further revelation in the days ahead regarding the Rapture of the Saints and His Second Coming. The meeting over, we all joined the rest of the congregation in the Carpenters Home Church and had a wonderful time with the Lord under the ministry of Charles and Frances.

The rest of our stay in the States was in Disneyland, Florida. We all had a marvellous holiday, taking in as much as we could in our short time there. Adrienne and Winona especially, loved America and everything American. The people were very friendly and warm towards us, nothing was too much trouble for them. The weather cooled down a bit, although temperatures were still in the high eighties, but the humidity had dropped a lot, thankfully. I was particularly impressed with the sheer professionalism of the American way of doing things. Waitresses, waiters, bellboys, anyone involved in serving the public did their jobs with a smile and a willingness to please that I have found in no other country. None of us wanted to leave when the time came, and it was with a very fond farewell that we bade the States goodbye when we boarded the big 747 that would take us back to England and home.

Tony Watson

We returned to the US a year later. This time the girls couldn't make the trip but Margaret's sister Mary and her husband Ken came with us. We ministered in several churches and meetings as the Lord led us and we were greatly blessed. We visited the Assembly of God Church in Brownsville, Florida, where in a mighty move of God, 100,000 souls have been saved in an eighteen month period since Father's day 1995.

We queued in temperatures of ninety degrees plus for four hours to get into a seven o'clock Friday evening meeting! The presence of God was awesome. When Rev. Steve Hill, a Missionary Evangelist of AOG gave the appeal for people to come forward and receive Jesus into their lives, hundreds of people responded. Later we were among the many people Steve and Pastor John Kilpatrick prayed for and laid hands on. As they did so, we knew instantly, we had received something new and powerful. This anointing brought a real conviction to believers about the need for genuine repentance, leading to greater righteousness and holiness in our lives. Our tears were many and we were deeply touched and further changed by the Holy Spirit.

On returning to England Margaret and I were given permission by our Pastors to 'take' the meeting that Sunday evening. Margaret and I duly shared our experiences of Brownsville and later prayed for about one hundred and fifty people, who all instantly fell out in the Spirit as we laid hands on them! The most wonderful thing happened however near the end of the meeting when Derek asked me to give an appeal for salvation. I spoke from the platform and said that I believed the Lord was telling me that there was someone in the meeting who felt lost, whose life was in a desperate mess. I said that they could have a fresh start, a new sheet if they came to Jesus as I had done! Two people responded, one a young back-slidden Christian youth and the other a middle-aged man who had never known the Lord. The man's name was Tony Watson, estranged from his wife and daughters, with a failing business. Margaret and I led them both through the prayer of salvation and rejoiced with them both and especially with Tony as he made his decision for Christ and a new life. We praised the Lord for him and we thought that was that! But God is able to do exceedingly, abundantly above all that we can ask or think, according to the power that works in us (Ephesians 3:20)!

We found out later that week, that Tony had been receiving treatment including surgery, for lymphatic cancer. Tony told us that all day Monday, he felt an electric tingling sensation throughout his body. On being examined by his specialist on Tuesday, however, no trace of the golf-ball sized growth in his groin could be found and he no longer has the cancer! We hadn't even prayed for Tony's healing, but God is a father who delights in giving His children good gifts, even if they are only just born again! Furthermore his business immediately recovered and he was re-united with his wife and family and they too asked the Lord into their lives, and became born again – Praise the Lord!

Chapter 16

The Way Back

by Margaret

'Then Peter opened his mouth and said: "In truth I perceive that God shows no partiality."' (Acts 10:34)

M alcolm and I believe that we are prime examples of the above scripture. This verse says that He is no respecter of persons, whilst society makes distinctions among people, God's love and grace are available for all and can be received by anyone.

My upbringing was rather different from Malcolm's. I was born into what is commonly called a 'Christian' family – my parents were very regular church goers and my sisters and I were brought up to go to church at least twice on a Sunday and two or three times during the week. Dad a retired Pastor, has talked in later years about his own background. His father was a lay preacher and very strict with his children, particularly in religious terms and as a result dad could only really follow in his footsteps.

As a small child I didn't question our way of living, it was different from friends I mixed with at school but it was OK. I had some good friends in the church, there were lots of activities for children: Sunday school outings to the seaside, a sports evening every week in the summer and I enjoyed participating in all that was going on. My parents sent me to piano lessons for a number of years and whilst at the time it was a chore I did learn to play reasonably well and later on joined a small group of musicians in the church.

We travelled around other churches playing and singing the Gospel. At around the age of ten years I was filled with the Holy Spirit and spoke in tongues; it went on for some hours and I remember even now that I experienced a joy that I had never known before. It is hard to believe that despite all this, I still deliberately turned my back on Jesus.

During my teenage years things changed and I began to be less than satisfied with life confined within church boundaries. I had observed my two older sisters, particularly Jane, the eldest of the three of us, and whose footsteps I wanted to follow in, rebelling against our strict upbringing and I was to be no exception. I think it was my developing interest in boys during the teenage years that finally took me away from church and into the apparent freedom of the world.

For twenty seven years I did what I wanted to do – I landed a good secretarial job in the film business at the age of twenty one which gave me the opportunity to travel on location to different places and of course I enjoyed the 'glamour' of the film industry. I worked for film director Bryan Forbes and his actress wife Nanette Newman and during the course of the ten years I was with them, met many famous actors and actresses: Peter Sellers, Peter Cook, Dudley Moore, Michael Caine, Roger Moore, Richard Chamberlain, Dame Edith Evans, Yul Brynner, Katharine Hepburn, and Danny Kaye to name a few.

During this period I married David, who I had known for about five years, and by the time I was thirty we had two children, Michael and Joanne. David was a good husband and provider – we had a nice house, we could afford to go on foreign holidays most summers and for a number of years everything seemed to go very well. I finished working for the Forbes after Joanne was born and for a couple of years was happy to stay home and look after the family.

By the time Joanne was three years old, and Michael was at school, I was looking for some work that would fit around the family. Party plan selling was very much in fashion at that time and I became involved with a company selling children's clothes. I was successful on a fairly modest scale and when David and I decided to move house from Burnham in Buckinghamshire to Camberley in Surrey, I asked the party plan company if I could open up a new area. They agreed, supplied a company car, and for the next couple of years business was good. However, the company I represented were ambitious and tried to grow too quickly and as a result, the effort I was able to make in the hours I had available did not bring the success I had previously enjoyed. I decided it was time to try something new.

I accepted a job with a small local company selling silk plants to shops and offices and became very friendly with the owners, in particular with Karen, and she and I spent many hours discussing 'the meaning of life'. It seemed a happy time, David and I had made lots of new friends in Camberley. He seemed settled in his job; I was content with my job, looking after the children, and getting involved in local activities.

Then David was made redundant. Although this came as quite a shock, in many ways our marriage grew stronger during that time – it seemed to bring us closer together as we joined forces to deal with the problem. It was only after he had found another job, some six months later, that the cracks in our marriage started to appear. There is no doubt that communication between us became less and less – I was frustrated with his apparent lack of interest in everything outside of his job, and as a result, I became increasingly involved in activities outside the home that didn't include him. How easy it is to see the mistakes we have made, after the event.

After I came back to the Lord, and especially since Malcolm and I have been married, the Holy Spirit has shown me so clearly how a lack of communication can bring about such drastic consequences. I believe women, particularly, are prone to allowing thoughts to come in which seem to support the negatives they are thinking about their partner.

If you don't stop them, a scenario can develop in your mind which can become almost total fabrication and lead to barriers being erected in the relationship. I found out too late that David's apparent lack of interest was due to concern and unhappiness with his new job. Unfortunately I was too busy thinking about myself to consider that he might have a valid reason for his behaviour.

I was unfaithful to my husband and eventually, after he had done all he could to save our marriage, we decided to part. By this time I was very independent and felt that I had no real need of men in my life, not on a permanent basis anyway and that I was quite capable of providing for myself and the children. Needless to say it was a very difficult time for our families and much hurt was caused by my determination to do things my way. My own parents tried to understand what had gone wrong but I was not interested in discussing the whys and wherefores. I didn't want to be questioned about my actions, after all, I was a free agent and didn't have to answer to anyone. At least, that is what I thought, I had forgotten all about God's universal law of sowing and reaping. Our very lives begin by the seed principle and every act of our lives since birth operates by that same principle, springing up from the good or bad seed we've sown, whether or not we have been consciously aware of our seed planting.

Something else I realise as I look back is that the Lord had His hand on my life. He provided a job for me with a computer company which paid and has continued to pay a very good salary. In the first instance this was to enable me to take care of my children so that, at least in monetary terms, they should not suffer too much. Another reason I am sure for my joining that company was because I was to have a relationship with a man who worked there which would result in my turning back to the Lord Jesus Christ.

Harry had been married twice but at the time I met him he was on his own and seemed to me to be a very nice guy. What I didn't realise until later was just how insecure he was which led to extreme possessiveness, particularly after a few drinks. Harry loved to buy me beautiful clothes but if any man paid me a compliment I would be accused of encouraging his attentions. It was a situation which grew worse. One day I had a picture which I now believe was the work of the Holy Spirit – it was a picture of a rag doll that had been well used and was now just thrown into a cupboard. The doll was kept in this cupboard and brought out to be played with now and again.

I realised that the time would come when that doll would

be discarded for good because its owner had finally reduced it to something that wasn't worth playing with any more. I knew that doll was a picture of me and I knew that was how I would end up if I didn't get out of this destructive relationship. I had lost a lot of weight, was drinking heavily and smoking up to forty cigarettes a day. One day whilst browsing in W.H. Smith the booksellers, that well known book by Norman Vincent Peale – *The Power of Positive Thinking* – caught my eye and I decided that this was what I needed. Life with Harry was pretty unbearable but still I clung to the relationship, in fact I seemed to be mesmerized by him and unable to escape. Although he would constantly find things to get angry about and the abuse was now physical as well as verbal, I seemed powerless to break the relationship. This was an all-time low for me and if the Lord Jesus Christ had not intervened when He did, I believe I would have ended up in a mental hospital.

As I started to read Peale's book, I was surprised to find that he frequently referred to verses in the Bible. By the time I had finished reading it, I thought I might as well start reading God's word for myself – I hadn't realised what positive things it had to say. At the same time I cried out to God to help me.

The relationship with my parents had been difficult during the years after my divorce from David – we seemed to have so little in common and although I went to visit, I never stayed very long. However, they knew I was looking for something. I can remember having conversations with my father about Karen's beliefs. Karen and I had stayed in touch after I stopped working for her and she had tried to help both David and me during our marital difficulties. She had become involved with the 'New Age' philosophy which seems to embrace bits and pieces of all religions. She believed we had all lived before, that each new life was an opportunity to 'get it right this time' and that God was a God of love. She didn't believe He was also a God of judgement. Karen was also involved with 'faith healing' and enjoyed a measure of success with the people who came to her. It was during my early friendship with her that I found out more about meditation, tarot card readings and other things of the occult. Dad was very definitely against all of this and told me to be careful what I became involved in. There is no doubt in my mind that the Holy Spirit kept me during that time. I was on the side-lines and always held back from having my cards read or from visiting fortune tellers; it just didn't seem right to me to get too involved. Our friendship came to a sudden conclusion after a lunch, sometime after I came back to the Lord, when I felt compelled to repeat several times the scripture in John 14 verse 6 where Jesus is saying to his disciples:

'I am the way, the truth, and the life. No one comes to the Father except through Me.'

This greatly disturbed Karen and we have had little contact since that time.

My parents began to notice a change in my conversation and when I started talking about the Word of God one day, dad asked me if I had made a decision to give my life back to Jesus. I said yes I had, and from that moment, having publicly as it were, declared my intention to allow Jesus Christ to run my life, I knew a peace and joy that had been missing for a very long time. Within a few weeks I was able to say goodbye to the destructive relationship with Harry, I was no longer held in its grip. You can see why we wrote in the introduction to this book that we believe in a simple gospel message:

Jesus Saves, Jesus Heals, Jesus Delivers

because that is exactly what Jesus has done for Malcolm and me!

It was a little while before I felt ready to face church. I spent the next year reading my Bible and getting to know God all over again.

My parents had more than once suggested that I should visit The King's Church in nearby Aldershot but when the time came and I felt ready to venture out, I decided that I wanted to find a local fellowship. I tried several different denominations before settling into a nearby Baptist church.

The people were nice and I already knew some of the members through my local tennis club.

I stayed there for six months, crying through most Sunday morning meetings as I believe the Holy Spirit dealt with some of the hurts within me. Then during the summer of 1991 I joined my sister Jane and a friend of hers, visiting from the States, my other sister Mary and her husband Ken, on a Bryn Jones Restoration Bible Week in Wales. What a week that was! I just revelled in the love of God for a whole week and knew I would never be the same again. I also knew that it was time for me to move on in terms of where I attended church. I mentioned this to my parents and they reminded me about King's Church in Aldershot, so this is where I made for the first Sunday I was home from Wales. The moment I walked into this 'green' place I knew that I had found my spiritual home.

Chapter 17

My Family and me ...
and Malcolm

by Margaret

It was towards the end of summer 1991 that I started attending King's Church on a regular basis. Derek Brown, the pastor, was an excellent teacher and the worship was beautiful. I made many new friends – Juliet Peatling was introduced to me almost as soon as I arrived that first Sunday morning and we became firm friends. I joined a local house group where I could share on a more intimate level and through the people in the group the Holy Spirit ministered to the deep hurts and disappointments that were still within me. I made friends with Christine Roche who I had been aware of before we met at the group. I had seen her dancing in church and been very blessed by her worship. I don't think I had realised before that there are many ways to worship Jesus and He loves to receive it, whether the praise is in word, song or dance.

Without my realising it God was making changes during those early days of reconciliation. He set my feet on a path that would bring about major changes to my basically selfish nature and change my attitude towards men. He revealed to me how He intended marriage to be. Marriage should be a reflection of the relationship between Jesus and His bride, the Church. Through those times of learning about tithing and giving, of being emotionally healed and set free, I realised more and more the truth of what the Bible says in Jeremiah 17, verses 9 and 10:

'The heart is deceitful above all things,
And desperately wicked;
Who can know it?
I, the LORD, search the heart,
I test the mind,
Even to give every man according to his ways,
And according to the fruit of his doings.'

With particular reference to marriage I made a vow to God one Sunday in church as I watched a couple holding hands and worshipping together. I realised what a blessing it would be to have a Christian marriage where the Holy Spirit was the third strand. I told God that if He ever gave me another husband I would be the sort of wife I should have been before, but never was. I wasn't actively seeking a husband, in fact the thought couldn't have been further from my mind at that time as my life had taken rather a different turn, but I would be reminded of that vow a couple of years later.

Towards the end of 1991 I decided to take out an endowment policy for £25,000. I already had a mortgage on the small house that the children and I shared, but I felt that this amount of money would enable me to pay off some minor debts, allow me to make changes in the house and ensure that, when the time came for Joanne to marry, I would have sufficient funds to take care of the expenses. The property had been surveyed for the policy, I had signed the papers and sent them back, everything was settled. In fact settled to the extent that I had already organised for a new power shower to be installed. For some reason though I had held on to the Declaration that came with the papers which gave a ten-day 'cooling off period' and the option of a change of heart.

That New Year's Eve I had collected mum and dad from Slough and taken them over to King's Church. As usual we had enjoyed a wonderful time of worship, ministry and prophecy and after taking them home I asked God if there was anything in my life that was not what He wanted. Immediately, into my mind came this endowment policy and the absolute certainty that I should not go through with it. I found the paper which allowed for the change of mind, completed and posted it the next day. (I was within 48 hours of the time limit.)

Not long afterwards God spoke to me about my parents and me moving together! This was not something I would ever have thought to do. I waited for several weeks before saying anything to anyone about this, I wanted to be absolutely sure that this was God's plan. I realised too, that if I had taken out the endowment policy, as originally planned, it would have had tremendous implications with regard to the financial arrangements.

Eventually I felt the timing was right and mentioned it to my parents and to my two sisters. All their reactions were different from what I expected and just confirmed to me that this was indeed of God. My sister Mary, who is normally quick to speak, said nothing; her husband Ken, who is normally slow to speak, immediately said, 'What a good idea;' my sister Jane telephoning from the States said, 'How exciting!'

There was a great deal to be sorted out – my house to sell, my parent's house to sell and the purchase of a suitable house that would be large enough for us all. However, when you are following a path that God wants you to walk in, there is a lightness in your step, you go forward in confidence, knowing that He walks before you!

Psalm 119 verse 35 says:

> *'Make me walk in the path of Your commandments,*
> *For I delight in it.'*

This was how we approached the project – for that is what it was. I cannot say that we experienced no difficulties at all but for the most part our plans proceeded smoothly. In fact the only major hiccup was due to me not paying attention to that 'still small voice'! I was wondering about a new mortgage and felt I should move from my existing lender. I had picked up information from several building societies, including one with which I had a small savings account. One day whilst walking past the doorway of this particular building society I had a nudge from the Holy Spirit about using them for the new mortgage.

However, I thought I should make sure I was getting the best deal and I decided to go through a broker, the same one that David and I had dealt with when we first moved to Camberley. He would shop around for me! (How often do we forget that the Holy Spirit has all knowledge and we don't need to double check that He has done His home-work.)

The house we had chosen needed planning permission for an extension in order for it to be suitable for us to buy so there was plenty of time for my house to be sold and the new mortgage to be arranged. However, we arrived at the summer of 1992, Mum and Dad, Mary and Ken, Jane and I were off once again to Bible week, when I discovered that the mortgage company were not able to deliver the new funds as agreed. This was just fourteen days before completion and two days before I was due to go on holiday!

I had a panic meeting with my solicitor, a very helpful lady who had been introduced to me through a Christian solicitor I knew from the Camberley Christian Business Fellowship, and she proceeded to telephone all the local building societies to see who could help me at such short notice. (Just to explain, the Camberley Christian Business Fellowship is a group of people of different denominations who spend one lunch break a week sharing with other Christians in worship, reading the word and praying. It's open to anyone who works in the Camberley area.)

The company which was able to supply the mortgage in the time available was the very one the Lord had nudged me about in the beginning! If only I had listened I would have saved myself all that hassle and money, since I had to pay again for surveyor's fees. As it was, during the week we were away I spent quite a lot of time each day in the local telephone box making calls back to Camberley to check that everything was proceeding as it needed to in order for me to move when I returned from holiday.

Another contact I had made during my years as Office Manager with the computer company was a local surveyor who worked for Carsons Estate Agents and who I had occasion to deal with many times in my company's efforts to find new premises. In a conversation during the early part of 1992 he told me he would be leaving his job and going to theological college. I was surprised, neither of us had realised that the other was a Christian and from that time we saw each other regularly at the Business Fellowship. I shared with those at the Fellowship about my plans to move and what would be needed in terms of additional accommodation for mum and dad. He introduced me to a friend of his called Jim Mainwaring who was an architect.

Jim became the architect for the building work at our new home. He paid great attention to detail and was so patient with us all as we slowly got the hang of putting our thoughts into words, so that he could convert our words into a drawing that would result in the best design possible for mum and dad. He made such good use of the available space and went on to project manage the building work in a very professional and competent manner. It was interesting too how we came upon our new home. There is no doubt that God directed me to this particular property – it was only the third house that I took mum and dad to see and we all knew straight away it was **the** one. Dad had given God a list of what he believed we wanted and this is what he asked for:

- A house that will suit Margaret;
- A garage that can be used to store things for Michael and Joanne during their time away from home;
- Space on the other side of the house to build an annexe (dad didn't want us to lose the garage);
- Close to a bus stop;
- Close to shops; and a final request –
- A workshop for dad.

We got all this and more! We have an excellent fish and chip shop just across the road, we have a garage close by where dad can walk to get his newspaper, we have a pub next door where the staff have been so helpful in supplying meals for mum and dad and if that isn't enough, recent roadworks have resulted in the bus stop being moved opposite the house! In August 1992, I moved into the house just in time for Joanne's 18th birthday. Mum and dad were to join me in December and the building work was completed for them to move into their own self-contained accommodation the following June.

One of the things that I wanted to do in the new house was to renew the bathroom. The house was about twenty years old and still had its original bathroom suite and tiles. I took sufficient mortgage to allow for this and some other improvements but one day, soon after moving in, as I stood in the bathroom, imagining how the new one would look, God spoke quite clearly and told me to pay the money off the mortgage and leave the bathroom. I believe I had learnt something from those previous experiences and knew that if God was telling me to do something it would be for my benefit, even if I couldn't see it clearly at the time. The first major improvement that Malcolm did in the house after we married was to install a new bathroom!

In the February of that year, Christine had invited me to her birthday party and this is where I met Malcolm. He told me later that he had first become aware of me when I had given a testimony at King's Church about the Lord healing me of tennis elbow and thought then that I seemed rather 'posh'. (This amused me since my father had paid for elocution lessons during my teenage years which the teacher eventually told him was a total waste of money!) We struck up a platonic friendship and over the next year played badminton together, attended various social gatherings and then in the March of 1993 had our first 'date'.

I had become increasingly attracted to Malcolm as I saw his spiritual maturity and the way he handled the many things that seemed to go wrong in his life. He didn't react as most people do, he didn't hold grudges, wasn't bitter and seemed able to trust God in everything.

In fact during the months prior to our marriage I asked God for a word picture that would describe Malcolm – I had been reading a book about the blessings of God and how He wants to bless us even to giving us our smallest request. My picture was of the mighty oak – this is how God sees Malcolm – his roots go deep and he has great spiritual strength.

Malcolm's two daughters, Adrienne and Winona were very nice to me. As time went on and I got to know the girls better, I could see how the Holy Spirit was keeping them. Many children from broken marriages have all sorts of problems, particularly insecurities, but these two have healthy emotions. In fact when Malcolm and I were contemplating marriage, the girls actually encouraged him to ask me!

As the relationship between Malcolm and me grew my parent's concern was obvious. My mother had been quite ill when she first moved to Camberley and she was struggling, probably more than any of us realised, with this major change to her life. They had lived in the house in Slough for fifty-six years and whilst mum knew the move was for the best, she was finding it hard to come to terms with her new situation.

Malcolm was really an unknown quantity to them. They knew he had been married twice before and that in itself would have been reason enough to question what I was doing. Apart from that, because of a car-accident, he didn't have a regular job and relied on God to supply his every need! It wasn't that mum and dad hadn't relied on God during the many years they had known Him but Malcolm trusted God in such a laid-back, confident way.

Dad was then hospitalised for a month with heart trouble and I have no doubt now, looking back on that period, that all in all it was an extremely worrying time for them both. Here they were, in a situation where they believed God had brought them and I was thinking of marrying this unsuitable man! However, God's word tells us in Romans 8 verse 28:

> 'And we know that all things work together for good to those who love God, to those who are the called according to His purpose.'

and as time went by and mum and dad got to know Malcolm better, they both grew to respect and love him. They would both say now that they don't know what we would all have done without him!

Michael and Joanne

My children of course would have their own tale to tell of those years of the family breaking up and the time that followed – the stormy relationship their mother had with Harry which on occasions disturbed them greatly. Only God can see the heart and only He knows the damage that was caused to Michael and Joanne by my selfish ways. However, God has given me His promise that He will save my children – the first time He showed me this was in a most dramatic way. Malcolm and I went to a Monday morning meeting where Johnny Barr, the Romany Evangelist who God has greatly used, was due to speak. During the worship God took me into His Presence – it was so beautiful. As I enjoyed the closeness He told me that this would be how He would save Joanne and others! I just cried, I was overwhelmed by God's goodness. It wasn't until some weeks later when reading an Arthur Wallis book where he gave a description of Revival that I realised that was exactly what God had shown me. Revival is Jesus coming close to people, to the point where they cannot resist Him, where their hearts melt before Him, as He is revealed by the Holy Spirit.

More recently, again during worship, I was thanking God for a miracle He had done for a young couple in the church – she was expecting a baby which for so long had seemed impossible but God had answered their prayers and given them the desires of their heart (Psalm 37:4). As I thanked Him for this miracle He told me He was going to do a miracle in my children's lives! Once again, the tears flowed as I was reassured by my Heavenly Father that His word is truth and,

> '... all the promises of God in Him are Yes, and in Him Amen, to the glory of God through us.'
>
> (2 Corinthians 1:20)

Michael and Joanne have seen a great change in me and I believe that to them, at this point in time, they would say that I am a hypocrite. How else would you explain the adultery and promiscuity in total contrast to a belief in the sanctity of marriage? I can only leave these things with the Holy Spirit and trust God. My mother has told me that during the years of my absence from the Lord, He made very real to her the story of the prodigal son and she continued to trust Him for my salvation throughout those twenty-seven years.

In many ways it has been easier for Michael to cope with what has happened in my life. He spent a year at High School in Texas before going to Imperial College in London and since graduating has worked for an international oil company who send him all over the world. Joanne, on the other hand, has been closer to home throughout most of this period. When I told the children about Mum and Dad and me sharing a house, they took the news quite well; Michael had already left home and only returned occasionally and Joanne was due to go to College to study to be a Diagnostic Radiographer.

What we didn't know then was that she would leave College after three months and come back home to live. Not only did this mean sharing the house with my parents but by the time she came back, Malcolm and I were going out together and Joanne made it clear that she didn't like him or want to have anything to do with him. She liked his daughters, but that was it. The major changes in me didn't help either. From her viewpoint I had changed from an independent woman who was at least equal to men, to one who was content to cook, clean and wait at table. That probably sounds extreme but it is most likely how Joanne would have viewed the change. It wasn't too many months before she moved out of the house and into shared rented accommodation. I know that she felt rejected and with all that had happened to her over the years I couldn't blame her for being resentful.

One of the things that I really thank God for is that Joanne came to our wedding. I had prayed about it and asked God to change her heart as she had been so definite about keeping well away. I know it was a difficult day for her but she came to the house in the morning, helped my mother to get ready, helped Adrienne and Winona to put their bridesmaids dresses on and then helped me to dress. I was very pleased to see her and I've enjoyed seeing the re-run of the wedding video just to watch Joanne!

Chapter 18

The Blessings of God

by Margaret

A fter Malcolm and I became engaged, I made a statement to him that I would sing to him at our wedding!
After I'd said it I began to wonder why I had so rashly
promised to sing in public – something I hadn't done in
years. I asked a friend of ours, Justin, to put something
together for me – he had written some beautiful worship
songs and I felt he would be able to capture the essence of
what I felt about God putting Malcolm and me together.
The song was finally completed and ready for me to learn a
week before the wedding! Talk about last minute, but I'm
learning that God often allows us to wait until the eleventh
hour before providing the solution. When I woke on the
morning of the wedding I felt very nervous and anxious but
as I looked to the Lord He reminded me of two of the fruits
of the Spirit – joy and peace. That is what He gave me that
day – I was able to sing to Malcolm and thoroughly enjoy
the occasion.

I didn't realise it then, but that song was to be the first of
many. The Holy Spirit has provided the words and music for
others and has brought me to a place where I no longer feel
so nervous about singing in front of people. After all, if we are
willing, God will use what little talent we have for His glory.
We shouldn't be too concerned about our lack of perfection.
Malcolm and I often refer to a comment the American
preacher Michael Brown, now at AOG Brownsville, made on
one of his visits to King's Church – 'we were all saved by an

imperfect gospel', meaning that we did not receive a perfect witness, but perhaps only heard a fragment of the message or that the person preaching did not fully explain the Gospel in all its detail, but imperfect as it was it was enough for the Holy Spirit to move on the Word and reveal the truth. I believe the scripture in 1 Corinthians 1:27 says it clearly:

> 'But God has chosen the foolish things of the world to put to shame the wise, and God has chosen the weak things of the world to put to shame the things which are mighty.'

Our friends at King's Church had suggested that we have a 'do it yourself' reception in view of the fact that we didn't have too much money available and offered to organise everything for us. I don't think they realised what was to be involved but we thank God for their love towards us and for all those people who so willingly provided for us, both in the church and outside.

If we needed confirmation that God had put us together, it came in various words and prophecies we received on our wedding day. Isn't it wonderful to know the Holy Spirit, and to be reassured by Him of God's purposes for our lives.

Malcolm and I spent our honeymoon in Israel. We weren't sure that we would be able to afford it but my sister Jane telephoned from the States a few weeks before our wedding and said that the family over there had collected together about £200 for us and she had felt to telephone and ask what we wanted to do with it! Malcolm and I believed it added to the confirmation we needed that we should visit Israel and so we made our plans. Malcolm had been there before and had told me about the Holy Spirit speaking to him so clearly and how there is a different atmosphere in that place.

The moment we arrived in Tel Aviv I knew what Malcolm had been talking about – it was a bit like walking into King's Church the first time – I felt so at home there. Nothing to do with the people, they don't have any time for each other, let alone for tourists, and the staff at the five-star hotel we stayed in were certainly not all giving five-star service!

However, they are God's chosen people and we are told to pray for the peace of Jerusalem.

It was just as Malcolm had said. The Holy Spirit spoke to me clearly whilst we were there – no question as to whether the voice was His or not. I knew when He spoke, there was no doubt in my mind at all. We didn't go there to visit the places made famous by Jesus although we did visit Galilee and walked to Jaffa where Peter had the vision of the sheet with the animals. In fact Malcolm and I walked there several times during our holiday, on one occasion enjoying an excellent curry and on another occasion, visiting Simon the Tanner's house, where Peter saw the vision and where we spoke with the Armenian Christians who now own the house.

Christ Church, near Jaffa Gate in Jerusalem made a big impression on me. I have never experienced worship like it. Malcolm and I were late arriving and were led upstairs to the small balcony at the back of the church. After the word had been given we started to praise and worship the Lord and it was so beautiful, both Malcolm and I stood there with the tears streaming down our faces. I believe we tasted a little bit of heaven!

A desire that God had put within me was for the gift of healing and at the first Bible week I attended, during a call for people to make a demand on the Holy Spirit, I asked for this gift. I was aware as I asked that I received something I hadn't experienced before. There was a manifestation in my body, a sense of warmth that went from top to toe. Although I was very slow to put the gift to work, I knew in a new way that God wanted to heal people **today**.

I mentioned earlier that I had been healed of tennis elbow – that had happened towards the end of 1991 during a service at King's Church when one of the pastors, Martin Hannington, had made a call for prayer and I just felt it was time I was healed. I hadn't gone forward for prayer before and although I believed God could heal I had for a while wondered whether he would heal me of something I had brought on myself through excessive sport!

My sister Mary had put me right on that one, so after having treatment with cortisone injections that only seemed to bring temporary relief from pain I was ready for God to do something. The minute Martin prayed for me I **knew** I was healed – a current of power went up my arm and although the pain didn't completely go for another week or so I kept declaring that God had healed me and told everyone I met! My friends at the tennis club were impressed, as they had seen me, either on court with a strap around my arm, or not playing at all because the pain was so bad. I was able to witness to them about the healing I had received from the Lord Jesus Christ.

I now had proof in my own body that God heals! Following this a young man at King's Chruch prophesied over me that God was saying I should go and do for others what He had done for me. When Malcolm and I started seeing each other we realised that we shared the same desires. We wanted to see the sick healed. God has been gracious and provided opportunities for us to minister His love to people through His Holy Spirit. He has shown us ways to pray, He has shown us that so often we pray about symptoms when we need to be addressing the cause of the symptoms. We thank Him that we are vessels fit for the Master's use (2 Timothy 2:21).

Malcolm and I are always thrilled to be able to lay hands on people and see them healed in Jesus' name. One lady we prayed for had an ankle problem. She was a runner and despite a lot of physiotherapy the ankle was weak and gave way frequently causing considerable pain. I invited her to come home with me one day so that Malcolm and I could pray for her. I remember that Malcolm prophesied over her, after commanding the bones and muscles to be healed and free from pain in Jesus' name. He prophesied that the ankle would be stronger than it had ever been. That was a year ago and she has had no problems with the ankle since and continues to run!

Malcolm and I returned from honeymoon to King's Church on Sunday 19th June 1994 to an outpouring of the Holy Spirit such as we had not known before. God has been working in us to prepare us for times ahead, difficult times we believe, when we need to be able to stand firm on His Word, knowing that all that matters is our salvation. The

Holy Spirit has been stripping away the outer layers, causing us to look at things in our lives which He wants us to discard. Habits, attitudes, reactions. He wants us to develop the fruit of the Spirit – because only the fruit will last.

Chapter 19

There's Always More to Learn
(Philippians 1:6)
by Margaret

O ne of the things I marvel at is the way God changes
us – from the inside out! As you will have realised from
my description of the way I lived my life in those 'independent' days, I was quite a feminist in my outlook and certainly
didn't hold with the biblical view of marriage that the
husband is head of the wife!

> *'For the husband is head of the wife, as also Christ is head of*
> *the church; and He is the Saviour of the body.'*
> (Ephesians 5:23)

We forget that God has all knowledge and all wisdom
therefore He knows far better than we do what gives us
security and makes us happy.

Before God could 'dump' me onto Malcolm He had to
make some changes to my basic nature and He did that by
revealing the truth of His Word to me. He showed me so
clearly that marriage as God intended it to be is a reflection of
Jesus and His bride, the Church. I also saw that in Genesis,
God made Eve to come alongside Adam and be his helpmeet
– once I could see the truth I wanted to walk in that truth
and so, as Malcolm and I started our married life together I
was given opportunity to put that truth into practice! It's
relatively easy to accept truth when it's shown to you but
it's sometimes a different matter to **walk according to the
truth**. I cannot say that it has always been easy to submit to

Malcolm's authority and I cannot say that I have reached perfection in this area yet but what I can say is that I have discovered the joy that obedience to God's Word brings. I have realised that God has given us direction for the way we should live for our good, to enhance our lives, to bring us pleasure, not only in this area of wives submitting to husbands but in all areas.

You might be thinking, well, this is a bit one-sided. What about the role of the husband! There's plenty said about the husband in Ephesians 5 but I believe that my responsibility is to be obedient to the word of God as it applies to me and I leave it to God to sort out the rest.

I want to give an example of how the active presence of the Holy Spirit inside marriage can bring about a better relationship. As we all know, going out with someone is different to living with them and not too long after Malcolm and I married I was struggling with an issue that I had tried to explain to Malcolm on several occasions. I realise, looking back, that I was trying to change him. I wanted him to see my point of view and then to change his ways to fall in line with me. It was a Sunday morning and I was feeling quite emotional about this particular issue. I tried once again to get Malcolm to at least acknowledge that I had a valid point. Instead, Malcolm walked away from me and into the bathroom whilst I was still in full flow! I went downstairs into the kitchen to make preparations for Sunday lunch and carried on complaining, but this time to God.

'Why can't Malcolm see how unreasonable he's being? Why can't he see my point of view?' etc. Suddenly God broke into this stream of complaints with two words:

'Who cares!'

It stopped me in my tracks and the realisation dawned that what God was saying was true – we can get taken up with the 'cares of this world' and really, whether I was right or wrong didn't make the slightest bit of difference – the whole issue was not worth being concerned about. God tells us:

> *'Be anxious for nothing . . . '* (Philippians 4:6)

He tells us that for good reason, I just wish I remembered it more often, **before** I become anxious. When Malcolm came out of the bathroom I went and apologised and explained how God had spoken to me. He just smiled and said, 'When I walked away from you upstairs, I said, "God, you'd better sort her out, because I can't." '

I'm so thrilled when God speaks to me, even if He is 'sorting me out'. Doesn't it show, once again, that He is interested in every detail of our lives. There have been many occasions when the Holy Spirit has brought us back together. One of the name's for Satan is 'Diabolos', which means 'the one who divides, separates and falsely accuses'. We see so much evidence of his handiwork in the world today, particularly in marriages. As Christians, let us not be ignorant of his devices and let us use God's Word and His power that He gives us through His Holy Spirit, to triumph again and again.

Not only has the Holy Spirit brought resolution to personal problems but has given us answers in situations where we are not sure what we should do. Malcolm and I are learning not only to pray together but to seek the Lord individually for confirmation of words and scriptures that He has given to us. The Holy Spirit never fails to make things clear to us – He might give me a word which needs clarification – Malcolm will ask for that clarification during his quiet time and will be given further insight. Sometimes Malcolm will ring me at work and say 'God has given me this word – will you ask Him for confirmation?' He **never** fails us – He always answers us and each step we take we are learning to commit to Him. We were given the following scripture at our wedding – the same verses came to us from two different people. I believe the Lord wanted us to take note of it!

> 'Trust in the LORD with all your heart,
> And lean not on your own understanding;
> In all your ways acknowledge Him,
> And He shall direct your paths.'   (Proverbs 3:5–6)

Postscript to Chapter 3 (see page 24)

Near the end of December 1995, Malcolm felt the Holy Spirit tell him to ring his old school in Taunton and enquire about a 'Reunion'. Now Malcolm had not had any contact at all with the school or his old schoolmates for over **thirty** years and the thought of a reunion never entered his head. But he discovered the number and rang anyway to find that the school was closed for the Christmas holidays, and then promptly forgot all about it!

Several months later he again felt that 'still small voice' telling him to ring the school and enquire about a reunion! He rang the school and enquired of the secretary who put him through to another department. When he enquired about a reunion the lady at the other end immediately said, 'Give us a chance! We've only just got the invitations back from the printers on Saturday and we haven't had time to send them out yet – the reunion is on 11th May. What was your date of birth?'

It transpired that the reunion organised was for Malcolm's year only – the first the school had ever arranged!

Malcolm asked the school secretary whether he could bring his wife to the reunion and she answered that unfortunately no wives or partners were allowed. Malcolm said that he would ignore this and take me anyway as we had arranged to visit Malcolm's mother on the way, since it was her 80th birthday next day. The invitation when it arrived clearly stated as if to underline the fact, **no wives or partners were to be brought**.

In the event Malcolm took me to his mother's house in Bristol that night and left me there with his mother as he continued on his way alone to his old school reunion in Taunton, a further forty miles away. Malcolm was to return afterwards and we would spend the night with his mother and next day have a birthday celebration with the rest of the family. His mother had been suffering from a badly swollen leg and just before bed-time I offered to pray for her. As I held her leg in my hands I looked up into her face and asked whether she would like to ask Jesus into her heart.

'Ooh yes, I would,' she said and I led her in the prayer of salvation. So on the eve of her eightieth birthday, Malcolm's mother was born again – what a present!

I lay awake in bed as Malcolm returned about midnight.

'Had a good evening, darling?' he asked.

'Guess what,' I replied. 'Your mother's given her life to the Lord, whilst you were out!'

After we had thanked the Lord for His goodness and kindness towards us and our families, Malcolm said that there **were** several wives and partners at the reunion and that it would have been no problem if I had gone with him.

Obviously God had other ideas! Next day at Malcolm's sister's local morning service the first thing Malcolm did was to get the microphone and tell everyone his mother was saved!

When we explained later what had happened to his sister Diane, she said, 'Well, God had to get Malcolm out of the way somehow, didn't He!'

Malcolm and Margaret

So that's it, the testimonies of two ordinary believers. How our lives fell apart, how the Lord Jesus Christ saved, healed, and delivered us. At this point we ought to relate how the Lord has been working in our family. Since Malcolm was saved in 1989, his father, sister, brother-in-law, his two daughters and his mother, have all prayed the prayer of salvation, asked Jesus into their lives and have been born again by the Spirit of God – praise the Lord! In his immediate family, there is only his brother, older sister and sister-in-law to go! In mine there are only two to go – we are believing for the Lord to save my son and daughter and are standing on the scripture:

> '...thus says the LORD:
> "Even the captives of the mighty shall be taken away,
> And the prey of the terrible be delivered;
> For I will contend with him who contends with you,
> And I will save your children."'   (Isaiah 49:25)

There's not much more to tell – this book is finished – or at least that's what we thought! We believe the Lord had other plans though and the second part of our story looks as though it may well be more fantastic, more incredible than the first!

PART TWO

'Out of Darkness into His Marvellous Light'

Chapter 20

The Bridegroom Returns for His Bride

by Malcolm and Margaret

L ike many other Christians we were fascinated by most teaching on the last days: the Books of Daniel and Revelation, the Great Tribulation, the Rapture and the Second Coming, the Millennium etc. were subjects of great interest. We were well acquainted with the 'end time' teachings of the New Zealanders, Barry Smith, George Curle, and others. We avidly read books, attended numerous lectures and listened to many tapes about how the Church would not have to go through the Tribulation, but instead be 'caught up' to be with the Lord before it started here on earth – Praise God!

When we came to write this book we did not intend to include anything at all about these subjects. After all what did a couple of nobodies like us know about such weighty matters! But increasingly Malcolm felt that the Lord was telling us to study them in more detail for ourselves. So we read more books, listened to more tapes and of course read the Word more. We read books by Tim La Haye, David Pawson, Dwight Pentecost, Hal Lindsay, David Wilkerson and others, including the Scofield Bible and Dake's Bible.

We discovered that there were two main schools of thought amongst Spirit-filled Christians. Those (including ourselves) who believed that the Rapture of the Church, the Body of Christ, would take place **before** the seven-year tribulation period and those who believed it would take place **after**. We soon discovered that it was a very thorny issue and that emotions could run high amongst those who held the two main opposing views.

On studying further the two opinions we began to become troubled over the **Pre-tribulation** Rapture teaching we had previously believed and assumed to be correct. We hadn't fully realised the implications of this particular doctrine concerning Israel. The simple fact was, that we had not checked out scripture for **ourselves**, but had gladly accepted the views and opinions of the 'experts'.

We examined the **Post-tribulation** view, expressed for instance by David Pawson MA BSc, the well-known English writer and biblical scholar, in his book, *When Jesus Returns*. But with its heavy emphasis on the suffering and passive endurance of the Church, 'Revelation is a manual for martyrdom' (p. 111) and with no mention of end-time believers going forth in the name of Jesus and in the awesome power of the Spirit – this view didn't exactly accord with our own experience of our mighty God. We didn't know what to believe, so Malcolm continued to study into the early hours on the subject and 'searched the Scriptures daily'.

We soon concluded that we needed to seek the Lord further on this problem, and after some weeks, Margaret felt that the Lord told her that He would give Malcolm 'insight and understanding' on the Rapture and **how** and **when** He will achieve this amazing translation of the Saints. Margaret felt too, that there was an important connection between the Marriage Supper of the Lamb, and the Rapture, and somehow sensed that the Spirit was prompting us to look at how old-style Jewish weddings were conducted in Israel, when Jesus was on the earth.

So we carried out some research and this is what we discovered:

The Marriage Supper

A Traditional Jewish Wedding at the Time of Jesus

Jesus was born a Jew and observed all the Jewish traditions and customs of His day, many of which are still carried on today. A traditional Jewish wedding of His day involved wedding celebrations which lasted seven days. These were special days of much feasting and celebration. Often the wine ran out before the seven days did.

> *'On the third day there was a wedding in Cana of Galilee, and the mother of Jesus was there. Now both Jesus and His disciples were invited to the wedding. And when they ran out of wine, the mother of Jesus said to Him, "They have no wine." Jesus said to her, "Woman what does your concern have to do with Me? My hour has not yet come." His mother said to the servants, "Whatever He says to you, do it." Now there were set there six waterpots of stone, according to the manner of purification of the Jews, containing twenty or thirty gallons apiece. Jesus said to them, "Fill the waterpots with water." And they filled them up to the brim. And He said to them, "Draw some out now, and take it to the master of the feast." And they took it. When the master of the feast had tasted the water that was made wine, and did not know where it came from (but the servants who had drawn the water knew), the master of the feast called the bridegroom. And he said to him, "Every man at the beginning sets out the good wine, and when the guests have well drunk, then that which is inferior; but you have kept the good wine until now."'* (John 2:1–10)

When a couple were betrothed in those days, the prospective Bridegroom paid the asking price of the Bride to the bride's father (1 Corinthians 6:20). Both parties then drank from a cup of wine, which signified the establishment of a covenant relationship.

> *'For this is my Blood of the new covenant, which is shed for many for the remission of sins. But I say to you, I will not drink of this fruit of the vine from now on until that day when I drink it new with you in My Father's kingdom.'* (Matthew 26:28–29)

The young man then returned to his father's house to prepare a bridal chamber in his father's house and build a new home for his bride on his father's land.

> *'In My Father's house are many mansions; if it were not so, I would have told you. I go to prepare a place for you. And if I go and prepare a place for you, I will come again and receive you to Myself; that where I am, there you may be also.'*
>
> (John 14:2–3)

The girl promised to him, wore a veil from that day on, so that any other potential suitor would know that the price for her had been paid.

> *'For you were bought at a price; therefore glorify God in your body and in your spirit, which are God's.'*
>
> (1 Corinthians 6:20)

Her part of the covenant was that she would remain faithful to him until his return. She waited at home with her bridesmaids, with bags packed, and lamps full of oil.

> *'Then the kingdom of heaven shall be likened to ten virgins who took their lamps and went out to meet the bridegroom. Now five of them were wise, and five were foolish. Those who were foolish took their lamps and took no oil with them, but the wise took oil in their vessels with the lamps. But while the bridegroom was delayed, they all slumbered and slept. And at midnight a cry was heard: "Behold, the bridegroom is coming; go out to meet him!" Then all those virgins arose and trimmed their lamps. And the foolish said to the wise, "Give us some of your oil, for our lamps are going out." But the wise answered, saying, "No, lest there should not be enough for us and you; but go rather to those who sell, and buy for yourselves." And while they went to buy, the bridegroom came, and those who were ready went in with him to the wedding; and the door was shut. Afterwards the other virgins came also, saying, "Lord, Lord open to us!" But he answered and said, "Assuredly, I say to you, I do not know you." Watch therefore, for you do not know neither the day nor the hour in which the Son of Man is coming.'*
>
> (Matthew 25:1–13)

For the custom was that the bridegroom normally returned suddenly and unexpectedly, usually in the middle of the night. The exact moment of the Bridegroom's return was always determined by his father who watched over his son to make sure that he was preparing a suitable dwelling place for himself and his bride. Only when the groom's father was satisfied with his son's work would he send his son to get his bride. In fact it was common for the bridegroom's friends to ask him, 'When are you going to get your bride?'

The bridegroom would answer, 'Only my father knows that day!'

> *'But of that day and hour no one knows, no, not even the angels of heaven, but My Father only.'*   (Matthew 24:36)

On that day as his father had instructed, he would arrive unexpectedly to 'steal' his bride, like 'a thief in the night!'

> *'For you yourselves know perfectly that the day of the Lord so comes as a thief in the night.'*   (1 Thessalonians 5:2)

The Jewish tradition was that **all** brides were abducted or 'stolen', usually in the middle of the night. Thus the brides-maids and friends had to stay with her until the groom returned with his friends. As no-one knew when that would be, it could be up to a year after the betrothal, someone would keep watch and shout when the groom's party approached (1 Thessalonians 4:16), so that the bride would have a little time to get dressed. She would then gather her things together and go out and meet him in the road together with her bridesmaids and friends (1 Thessalonians 4:17).

> *'For the Lord Himself will descend from heaven with a shout, with the voice of an archangel, and with the trumpet of God. And the dead in Christ will rise first. Then we who are alive and remain shall be caught up together with them in the clouds to meet the Lord in the air. And thus we shall always be with the Lord.'*   (1 Thessalonians 4:16–17)

He would then quickly take his bride and her party back to the bridal chamber which he had been preparing in his father's house, and the bride and groom would go inside alone and shut the door. The marriage celebrations could not begin until they had consummated the marriage.

> *'Let us be glad and rejoice and give Him glory, for the marriage of the Lamb has come, and His wife has made herself ready.'*　　　　　　　　　　　(Revelation 19:7)

The groom had a friend who would stand outside the door of the bridal chamber and wait until the groom told him through the door, that they had consummated the marriage. Only then were they deemed to be married.

> *'He who has the bride is the bridegroom; but the friend of the bridegroom, who stands and hears him, rejoices greatly because of the bridegroom's voice.'*　　　　　　　(John 3:29)

The Bride had now become a Wife. Now the marriage celebrations could begin. Eventually the Husband and Wife made an appearance at the celebrations and their wedding feast (Marriage Supper) continued.

> *'Then he said to me, "Write: 'Blessed are those who are called to the marriage supper of the Lamb!'"'*
> 　　　　　　　　　　　　　　　　　　　(Revelation 19:9)

At the end of the seven days, the marriage supper over, the couple left the husband's father's house. Now legally married, they made the journey to their own home, the husband leading, with his wife dutifully following.

> *'Then I saw heaven opened, and behold, a white horse. And He who sat on him was called Faithful and True, and in righteousness He judges and makes war. His eyes were like a flame of fire, and on His head were many crowns. He had a name written that no one knew except Himself. He was clothed with a robe dipped in blood, and His name is called The Word of God. And the armies in heaven, clothed in fine linen, white and clean, followed Him on white horses.'*
> 　　　　　　　　　　　　　　　　　(Revelation 19:11–14)

This wonderful description of a typical Jewish Wedding gave us fresh insight into how Jesus the Bridegroom will return for His Bride, His Body, the Church. But we still had many questions that needed to be answered.

(Revelation 19:7) describes the wedding of the Lamb taking place in **Heaven** (i.e. The Bridegroom's Father's house!)

How is this possible? How and when do the Saints get there?

Chapter 21

The Bride Becomes a Wife
by Malcolm and Margaret

T he voice of the great multitude says:

> *'Let us be glad and rejoice and give Him glory, for the marriage of the Lamb **is come**, and His **wife** has made herself ready.'*   (Revelation 19:7)

(Note that the term *'wife'* appears for the first time in the Book of Revelation.)

The Hebrew word *'ishshah'* or the Greek, *'gunê'*, can mean 'bride', 'wife' or 'woman'. In the announcement, *'the marriage of the lamb is come'*, the use of the Greek *'elthen'* in its aorist tense for 'is come', signifies 'a finished, completed act', indicating that the marriage has indeed **been** consummated. This confirms that the context of *'ishshah'* in this scripture means **'wife'**.

'Bride' – 'wife' – 'woman' – what difference does it make?

Well, the use of the word 'wife', instead of 'bride' or 'woman', can mean only one thing, that a marriage **has taken** place and according to the old Jewish custom, that marriage has been consummated! **Never** at any time, except **after** a wedding ceremony can a bride be described as a **'wife'**. Not only is it a description of a spouse, it is also a **legal** term!

> *'And to her it was granted **to be** arrayed in fine linen, clean and bright, for the fine linen is the righteous acts of the saints.'*   (Revelation 19:8)

> *'And the armies in heaven, clothed in fine linen, white and clean, followed Him on white horses.'*   (Revelation 19:14)

Who followed Jesus? – *His Wife!*
From Where? – *Heaven!*
Where To? – *To Earth!*

'The Armies in Heaven'

David Pawson in his book, *When Jesus Returns* (p. 16), compares the *'Parousia'* (the return of the Lord), to the people of a city going out to meet a visiting king and returning to that city with him. But in our humble opinion, the **definitive** comparison and surely the most appropriate one, is of the Jewish **Bridegroom**, Jesus, returning for His **Bride**, the Church and of her going out to meet Him, returning with Him to His Father's house for the Wedding and Marriage Supper!

Scripture describes Jesus returning from Heaven to earth with ten thousands of his saints. Jude 14–15 states:

> *'Now Enoch, the seventh from Adam, prophesied about these men also saying, "Behold the Lord comes with ten thousands of His saints, to execute judgement on all, to convict all who are ungodly among them of all their ungodly deeds which they have committed in an ungodly way, and of all the harsh things which ungodly sinners have spoken against Him."'*

The traditional Post-tribulation rapture view holds that the saints referred to in Jude, must be the angels who accompany Jesus on His return to earth. They believe that for the believers, the rapture will be a quick 'up and down' event. **Up** to meet the Lord in the air, followed by **down**, i.e. an immediate return to earth, for the Marriage, which they say will take place on earth upon the Lord's return! **At no stage** do they envisage that Jesus takes the believers to Heaven.

However, the word 'saints' is literally 'Holy Ones' (Greek: *'hagios'*) and can refer to believers **as well** as angels. So these saints who accompany Jesus on His return to earth, at the

Parousia, could well be a description of believers, or angels or both! This does not get us very far. Jude is not specific enough for us to be absolutely certain. So in order to be certain that the term 'saints' most certainly includes believers – it must be proved from scripture on separate grounds in addition to those found in Jude 15.

We judged that the case would be proven if it could be established beyond question that the, 'armies in heaven', referred to in Revelation 19:14 who follow Jesus to earth, are composed **exclusively of believers** and that this description of them cannot possibly refer to angels.

So, we re-examined scripture and found that the case for stating that 'believers' **will** accompany Jesus on His return to earth and that these believers will follow Jesus out of heaven, can indeed, be well established from scripture.

We discovered that we could:

1. Establish from scripture, that the context of the believers presence in heaven is for a particular purpose confined **'exclusively to believers'** which cannot possibly be extended to, or be fulfilled by angels.
2. Establish from scripture, that this purpose, is described as being fulfilled **in heaven**, and **nowhere** else, **before** Christ returns to earth.
3. Establish from scripture that amongst the saints or 'holy ones', who are with Jesus, when He returns to earth will be these very believers, who are described in terms that cannot apply to angels. We maintain, that in our opinion, the establishment of points 1, 2 and 3 is indeed confirmed by scripture, in the following passages.

Point 1

(a) Revelation 19:8

'And to her was granted **to be** arrayed in fine linen, clean and white, for the fine linen is the righteous acts of the saints.'

(b) Revelation 19:14

'And the armies in heaven, **clothed** in fine linen, white and clean, followed Him on white horses.'

Here we have two separate references to the 'bride' or 'wife' of the Lamb and 'the armies in heaven' which refer to the wearing of a unique type of fine linen:

> *'for the fine linen is the righteous acts of the saints.'*
> (Revelation 19:8)

Some translations read *'the righteousness of saints.'*

The term *'righteous acts'* or *'righteousness'* is from the Greek word *'dikaima'*, meaning 'the product or result of being justified by God. The rights or claims which one has before God when he becomes His son by faith through Christ.'

In the context of (Revelation 19:8), the Greek term used is *'dikaimata'*, meaning the **'legal rights of saints'**. It is only **believers** who can obtain legal rights and who are **justified** and **sanctified** through **faith** in Jesus Christ – not angels. Those who are qualified and legally entitled to wear this unique fine linen, clean and white, therefore, **can only** be believers, not angels.

Angels simply cannot qualify nor obtain the legal right to wear this unique apparel, 'fine linen, clean and white' and accordingly, there is no reference anywhere in scripture of it being worn by angels. Therefore the description of the 'wife' or 'bride' and the 'armies in heaven' who followed Him 'out of heaven' (Revelation 19:11), can refer **only** to believers, clothed in fine linen, **not** angels.

The first reference (a), states that permission had been given (granted) for her, *'**to be** arrayed in fine linen, clean and white.'*

The second, subsequent reference (b), states that, *'the armies in heaven, **clothed** in fine linen, white and clean, followed Him on white horses.'* These separate references to the bride or wife and the armies in heaven are obviously (a) **before** and (b) **after** illustrations of the same category of saints, i.e believers – not angels.

The only other possible explanation, is that the armies in heaven comprise a **second** category of believer, unrelated to the bride or wife. We discount this option as illogical and not borne out by the evidence of the scriptures concerned. We must conclude therefore that the group of people referred to in Revelation 19:8 and Revelation 19:14 are absolutely **one and the same**.

To re-cap then:

The first description is that of the bride or wife **before** she is arrayed or clothed in fine linen. The second description is that of the bride or wife (the armies in heaven) **after** she is clothed or arrayed in fine linen.

Revelation 19:14 describes *'the armies **in heaven'*** (or, His wife) as being clothed or arrayed in fine linen **before** they follow Him.

Revelation 19:11 describes heaven being opened and Jesus mounted on a white horse. Revelation 19:14 states that *'the armies in heaven, **followed** Him on white horses.'*

Point 2

If Jesus is described as being in heaven, it means that those who 'followed Him', must have been in heaven too!

It is this army of saints (His wife), *'clothed in fine linen, white and clean'* (which as we have seen, cannot be granted to angels), which comprise the **believers**. Their **location** is described as being **in heaven**.

Point 3

Further confirmation, that the believers do indeed return with the Lord, if more were required, is to be found in Revelation 17:14 where the armies with the Lord, at the battle with the ten kings at Armageddon (see Appendix A) are described.

> *'These will make war with the Lamb, and the Lamb will overcome them, for He is Lord of lords and King of kings; and those who are **with Him** are called, chosen, and faithful.'*

Christ's designation here is, 'Lord of lords and King of kings', the same one used to describe Him in Revelation 19:16, immediately after He leaves heaven at the head of His armies (the believers), when He and they descend to earth. His title is the same, logically His armies must be the same.

This is indeed confirmed by the descriptions applied to those 'with Him':

> '*those* **with Him***, are* **called***,* **chosen** *and* **faithful***.*'

(In the Greek: '*kletos*', '*eklektos*', '*pistos*'.)
- '*Kletos*': 'The called ones, *kletoi*, having conformed to God's saving purpose'.
- '*Eklektos*': 'Related to *eklegomai*, giving favour to the chosen subject, keeping in view a relation to be established between him and the object'.
- '*Pistos*': 'One believing in the gospel of Christ, a believer, a Christian'.

These adjectives in this context can only apply to those saints known as, 'the armies in heaven,' i.e. believers, not angels.

In the whole of scripture, there is no location or occasion, other than **in heaven** and **before** following Jesus out of heaven, where believers are described as being arrayed in fine linen, clean and white. We believe then, we have established from scripture, that the granting of the wife/armies in heaven to be arrayed in fine linen, clean and white, is reserved exclusively for **believers**. We have no doubt that angels do indeed accompany Jesus **and** the believers at His Second Coming, but we believe that we have proved, from **scripture**, that the term 'saints', or 'holy ones' who accompany Jesus at His Second Coming most certainly includes **believers**.

Indeed it is the believers who **exclusively** comprise, '*the armies in heaven*'.

So if the location of the 'clothing', of the saints, is accepted, as being in **heaven** and not on earth, then where is the location of the **Marriage**?

Is it in heaven **before** Jesus returns, or on the earth **after** Jesus returns?

The Location of the Marriage of the Lamb

Re-statement

There is no location or occasion, in scripture, other than **in heaven** and **before** following Jesus out of heaven, where believers are described as being arrayed 'in fine linen, clean and white'.

As we have established, the granting of the wife/armies in heaven to be arrayed in fine linen, clean and white, is reserved **exclusively for believers**.

We suggest therefore that it is logical to conclude that the clothing of believers in this unique apparel, forms an **integral** part of the Marriage ceremony, at which believers (the Bride) are married to the Lamb. These saints (the wife/ armies in heaven), are described as being 'clothed in fine linen', **before** they descend to earth with the Lord. This being the case, the Marriage of the Lamb must have **already** taken place in heaven.

All believers, both the living and the dead, **must** therefore have to be present in heaven for their marriage to the Lamb. If not, i.e. if there is a **single** believer still present on earth, either dead or alive, when Jesus returns with the 'armies in heaven', then that believer would have 'missed' the Marriage in heaven, would have also missed being 'clothed in fine linen, clean and white,' and could not therefore have joined the 'armies in heaven'! There would thus have to exist a **second** category of believer, a concept which we have already stated, we do not believe to be scriptural!

Summary

If after considering these scriptures if one still maintains that Revelation 19:7 doesn't explicitly state that the marriage takes place in heaven, then surely it must be agreed that we have at least established from scripture that the **clothing** of **all** the believers in their unique fine linen, most certainly does take place there! If so, then it must be conceded, that it is logical to conclude that whilst the believers were there in heaven, it is inconceivable that they would not have been married to the Lamb at that time.

If the location of the marriage and 'clothing', of the saints, is accepted, as being in heaven and not on earth, then **how** do **all** the saints (in this case believers, not angels) get there and **when**?

What does scripture tell us?

Matthew 24:30 states:

> *'Then the sign of the Son of Man will appear in heaven, and then all the tribes of the earth will mourn, and they will see the Son of Man coming on the clouds of heaven with power and great glory.'*

Mark 13:26–27, describing the Second coming immediately after the tribulation writes:

> *'Then shall they see the Son of Man coming in the clouds with great power and glory. And then He will send His angels, and gather together His elect from the four winds, from the farthest part of the earth to the farthest part of heaven.'*

These passages are generally accepted by both Pre- and Post-Tribulationists doctrines to refer to the **Second Coming** of Jesus Christ.

But isn't this description of the 'gathering of the elect' strikingly similar to the events described in 1 Thessalonians 4:16, 17, where the term 'rapture', is derived? (Greek: *'harpazo'*, snatch, to seize to oneself by force.)

> *'Then we who are alive and remain shall be caught up together with them in the clouds **to meet the Lord in the air. And thus we shall always be with the Lord.'***

Significantly the Greek word 'to meet' (*'apantesis'*), is used in this context to convey the meaning of leaving a place and going to meet someone who is coming towards you.

We now believed that we were able to establish quite conclusively from scripture, that **all** the believers will indeed accompany Jesus **at** His second coming, **after** the marriage supper in heaven. But exactly how and when still remained a mystery. We searched the scriptures, but could not discover the answer we sought.

Post-tribulationists have the following dilemma; they believe that the rapture of the saints and the second coming are virtually the same event. They have no problem with the **concept** of a rapture, i.e. the resurrection of the dead in Christ, incorporating the translation of those who are alive at his coming. But they cannot understand how the Marriage of the Lamb can take place in heaven as well. It's as if the saints have to be in two places at the same time!

On the other hand, the Pre-tribulationists not only accept the rapture, they refer to it as their, 'blessed hope':

> '...looking for the blessed hope and glorious appearing of our great God and Saviour Jesus Christ.'   (Titus 2:13)

But they arbitrarily separate the 'blessed hope' from the 'glorious appearing' and maintain that the rapture and the second coming are two separate and distinct events, separated by a period of seven years. These seven years are supposed to equate to seven days, the prophetic 'week' of Daniel, which they believe the church will spend in heaven whilst the tribulation takes place on earth. They explain that those 'who are alive and remain' is the description of the church, at the time of the rapture, before the tribulation. Their explanation of those believers who are alive at the second coming after the tribulation is over, is that these are two groups of people who have become believers during the tribulation. Gentile believers – whom they refer to as 'Tribulation Saints' – and Jewish believers – the remnant of Israel. They reason that because these groups were on earth during the tribulation, they could not possibly have been present at the Marriage of the Lamb, which takes place in heaven. These two groups therefore **must** form second and third categories of believers who cannot be members of the Bride or Wife. Unless of course any believers from either of these two groups die during the tribulation, whereupon they then join the previously raptured church in heaven and then in fact do become members of the Bride or Wife! Complicated, or what?

Both doctrines can quote reams of scripture in support of their beliefs and the two opinions are apparently irreconcilable. Some of the arguments hinge on the interpretation of just one small Greek word, *'ek'* and its usage as described in

Chapter 3 of Tim La Haye's book, *No Fear of the Storm* (published by New Wine Press, 1992).

To simple believers like Margaret and me, it is rather remininiscent of the two nations in Jonathan Swift's, *Gulliver's Travels*; the 'Big enders' and the 'Little enders', that went to war over which end of a boiled egg was the correct one to open!

So which doctrine is correct?

There **has** to be a correct interpretation of scripture.

Both doctrines cannot be correct! Maybe **neither** is correct!

Chapter 22

Peter's Time Formula –
The Rapture 'Code'
by Malcolm and Margaret

S everal months passed by and we were no nearer an
answer to the Pre-/Post-Tribulation dilemma, until one
day, quite suddenly, the words of Peter (2 Peter 3:8) were
quickened to Malcolm over and over by the Spirit, until –
the 'penny dropped'.

We believe without doubt, that God has revealed to us,
incredible as it may seem, the amazing answer as to the **how**
and the **when** of the Rapture of the Saints and His Second
Coming!

We do not know why the Lord should have chosen to reveal
this to us. Some people have said, 'Who do you think you are?
I've studied the Bible for years and God has never shown me
what you claim!' As we have said we are not academics
or Bible scholars. As Frances Hunter would say we are just
'do-nothing, no account, nobodies', but we share the following with all who would keep an open mind and we simply ask
that they might consider it prayerfully.

It is significant that an unusual phrase used by Peter when
he wrote of the return of the Lord was:

> *'But, beloved, do not forget this one thing, that with the Lord*
> *one day is as a thousand years, and a thousand years as one*
> *day.'*   (2 Peter 3:8)

Here Peter not only refers to Psalm 90 verse 4, but builds
on it adding, *'a thousand years as one day'*.

We believe the Spirit showed Malcolm, that this phrase is **nothing less** than a simple code or mathematical formula, describing how time passes on earth from God's viewpoint.

Taken literally, it means that if one were to spend one earth day, in heaven (i.e, 'with the Lord'), then **less than a quarter of a second** would elapse, here on earth, incredible though that may seem!

The calculations involved are elementary. Anyone with an ordinary pocket calculator, a pencil and a sheet of paper can work them out!

However to be absolutely sure, Malcolm had them verified by Dr Jim AlKhalih of the Department of Physics at Surrey University, Guildford, England, who confirmed that the formula is mathematically correct. Dr Jim AlKhalih is an expert in Quantum Physics and a non-believer, so he has no axe to grind. Before he met Malcolm, Dr AlKhalih didn't even know what the 'Rapture' was. Needless to say, he sure does now! Dr AlKhalih considered carefully what Malcolm had to share and explained that Quantum Physics although a relatively new science, was based on concepts that, Albert Einstein, amongst others, had proposed earlier this century. Dr AlKhalih had no problem interpreting Malcolm's calculations. After studying the data for a few minutes or so, Dr AlKhalih expressed the following simple mathematical formula, 'on the back of an envelope':

$$\text{T.H.}/\text{T.E.} = 365{,}000$$

'1 day of earth time (in heaven) is equal to 1000 years of earth time (in heaven) and 1000 years of heaven time (on earth) is equal to 1 day of earth time (in heaven).'

It appears more complicated than it really is, but its literal meaning is:

'Time elapses 365,000 times faster on earth than it does in heaven!'

It is the **exact** mathematical translation of Peter's words in 2 Peter 3:8.

That's why Margaret and I, call it, '**Peter's Time Formula**'!

You may say, 'But surely heaven is outside time!' That's
what we thought too! But it's not our formula – it's God's;
and if He says *'with the Lord one day is as 1000 years and 1000
years as one day'* – then that's good enough for us!

Dr Alkalih says the principle of time flowing at different
rates in different places within our physical Universe,
expressed by Einstein's Theory of Relativity, is well understood today and accepted by all Quantum Physicists.

'Peter's Time Formula': T.H./T.E. = 365,000

Earth	Heaven	Earth	Heaven
1 day	1000 years	1000 years	1 day
1.44 mins	1 year	1 year	1.44 mins
0.24 secs	1 day	1 day	0.24 secs
0.0096 secs	1 hour	1 hour	0.0096 secs

When we were writing this book, we wrote to David
Pawson, sharing what we believed the Lord had shown us.
His reply was somewhat sceptical, but he concluded his
letter by saying that we **could** be right in our theory!

Imagine then how thrilled and excited, Margaret and I
were several months later, when we discovered that James
Reid, an American Scientist and a Christian had published
the following in his book, *'God, the Atom and The Universe*,
Zondervan Press, 1968, p. 64:

'Time slows down as speed increases. If spacemen were
travelling at or near the speed of light, and beamed their
TV cameras on planet earth, over four days of our actions
would be squeezed into one second of their time – they
would only have to watch **one** of their **days** to see a
thousand years of earth's history pass across their tube.

Whilst this ratio is the same as that given in the Bible
for God's time, it is important to note another fact
inherent in the Bible's statement. God can take either
view, or exist in either time scale. He can move in and
through time as freely as man can in his three dimen-
sions. Finally this verse not only shows that the Bible
(and God) knew that time can vary, but seems to

indicate that God expected man to learn of the fact one day.'

James Reid's Formula

2 Peter 3:8: 1000 years = 1 day   365,000 days   1 day

Ratio. 365,000/1   3,650,000 secs   10 secs

$$60\frac{\text{secs}}{\text{min}} \times 60\frac{\text{min}}{\text{hr}} \times 24\frac{\text{hrs}}{\text{day}} \times 30\frac{\text{day}}{\text{mth}} = 2,592,000 \text{ secs/mth}$$

$$\frac{3.65 \times 10^6}{2.6 \times 10^6} \bigcirc \text{ secs}   1.4 \text{ mths} = 10 \text{ secs}$$

.14 mths = 1 sec   4.2 days in one second

The method of James Reid's calculations is rather more scientific than Malcolm's, but his conclusion is identical to Malcolm's and confirms that, *'with the Lord a day is as a thousand years and a thousand years as a day.'*

> 'Man's ability to travel at speeds near those of light may be closer than most of us expect. This was shown by a recent investigation to determine speeds that might have to be simulated in future plasma-tunnels. The forecast was started by first determining the rate at which man had been increasing his speed of travel this century, with particular emphasis on the speeds of aircraft, rockets and spacecrafts. The general results of this are shown in Figure 1 (p. 170). Extrapolating the resulting curve to the speed of light indicates that if man continues increasing the speed at which he can travel at the same rate as in the past, he will be able to reach the speed of light by the year 2018.'
>
> (James Reid: Associate Fellow in the American Institute of Aeronautics, Member of the Franklin Institute; ASME, ASA, BSME, Drexel Institute USA)

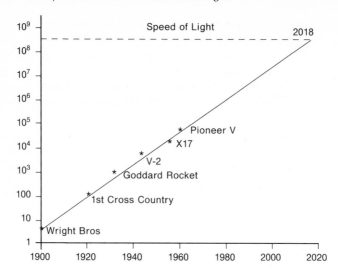

Figure 1 *Man's Increasing Speed.*

James Reid's description of four days being squeezed into one second, equates exactly with a picture the Lord gave Malcolm of a funnel, with the widest part representing time in heaven and the narrowest part representing time on earth:

> *'By the mouth of two or three witnesses every word shall be established.'* (2 Corinthians 13:1)

So what does it all mean and how can it affect the Rapture of the Saints?

The Effect of Peter's Time Formula on a Pre- or Mid-tribulation Rapture

1. If the rapture were to take place **before** or even **during** the tribulation and the raptured saints spent the equivalent of 7 **earth** years in heaven (for the duration of the tribulation), then only 10.08 minutes (1.44 minutes × 7) would have elapsed on earth.

2. They would **not** be away from earth **long enough** to escape the tribulation.

3. The raptured saints, although glorified and indestructible, would return to earth **too early** for the Second Coming – which takes place **after** the tribulation!

4. If they spent 7 **heaven** years in heaven, then they would definitely escape the tribulation – but 2.6 million years would have elapsed on earth! They would return **too late** for the Second Coming!

So **according to Peter's Time Formula**:

A Pre- or even Mid-tribulation Rapture of the Saints, in order to escape the tribulation, is simply **not possible**.

The Effect of Peter's Time Formula on a Post-tribulation Rapture

1. If the raptured saints were to attend the **seven day** Marriage Supper of the Lamb (the traditional Jewish Wedding) spending the equivalent of 7 earth **days** in heaven, then return to earth with the Lord – a period of only **1.68 seconds** (7 × 0.24 seconds) would have elapsed on earth!

2. To an observer on earth, the Rapture and the Second Coming would take place almost **simultaneously**, but the Raptured Saints, would experience seven earth days in heaven – **between** the Rapture and the Second Coming!

3. As the Second Coming, according to scripture is described as taking place **after** the 'tribulation of those days', and according to **Peter's Time Formula** the Rapture is practically contemporaneous with the Second Coming (the two events separated by a mere 1.68 seconds), it must mean therefore that the Rapture of the Saints must **also** take place **after** the 'tribulation of those days'.

So, **according to Peter's Time Formula**:

The only possible 'window of opportunity' for the Rapture to occur, is indeed **after** the tribulation and immediately **before** the Second Coming!

If this is correct, then believers will indeed have to go through the tribulation.

- But who wants to go through the tribulation?
- How will believers survive? Would there be anyone left alive to Rapture?
- How long exactly does the Great tribulation last?

These were just some of the many questions we had that needed to be answered.

Duration of the Great Tribulation

Some describe The Great tribulation as lasting for seven years, but nowhere in scripture is it described as lasting seven years! It is referred to in the book of Daniel as lasting *'time, times and half a time'*, or forty-two months, 1260 days, or three-and-a-half years.

Jesus Himself tells us **exactly** how long the Great tribulation will last:

> *'Therefore when you see the "abomination of desolation," spoken of by Daniel the prophet, standing in the holy place (whoever reads, let him understand), then let those who are in Judea flee to the mountains. Let him who is on the housetop not come down to take anything out of his house. And let him who is in the field not go back to get his clothes. But woe to those who are pregnant and to those with nursing babies in those days! And pray that your flight may not be in winter or on the Sabbath. For then there will be great tribulation, such as has not been since the beginning of the world until this time, no, nor ever shall be.'*
>
> (Matthew 24:15–21)

The timing of the setting up of the abomination of desolation, spoken of by Daniel is described in Daniel 12:11:

> *'And from the time that the daily sacrifice is taken away, and the abomination of desolation is set up, there shall be one thousand two hundred and ninety days.'*

> *'Then he shall confirm a covenant* (treaty) *with many for*
> *one week* (seven years)*;*
> *But in the middle of the week*
> *He shall bring an end to sacrifice and offering.*
> *And on the wing of abominations shall be one who makes*
> *desolate,*
> *Even until the consummation, which is determined,*
> *Is poured out on the desolate.'* (Daniel 9:27)

Clearly then in the middle of the seven year treaty period, the daily sacrifice is taken away and the abomination of desolation is set up.

According to the words of Jesus this signals the beginning of the great tribulation which lasts for the second half of the seven years, i.e. 1260 days.

So Pre-tribulationists seeking to equate the Rapture and the Marriage of the Lamb with Daniel's prophetic 'week' of seven years, and the seven days of the Marriage Supper, can in reality only equate a period of three-and-a-half years.

This would necessitate the Marriage Supper to be of three-and-a-half day's duration, not seven! The traditional Jewish Wedding was **always** seven days! This poses serious problems for the Pre- or Mid-tribulation theorists.

The Hour of Trial

The promises to the 'faithful' church (a 'type' of the church in Philadelphia) described in Revelation 3, include:

> *'See I have set before you an **open door**.'*

> *'I also will keep you from the **hour of trial** which shall come upon the whole world, to test those who dwell on earth.'*

The phrase, *'those who dwell on earth,'* is used to describe mankind in **opposition** to God (Revelation 6:10; 8:13; 11:10; 13:3, 8, 12, 14; 14:3, 6; 17:2, 8).

We asked ourselves the question, 'Is the "hour of trial that is going to come upon the whole world," a reference to the great tribulation?'

We further considered that perhaps a more pertinent question and one more likely to provide the answer should be: 'Is there any reference elsewhere, in the book of Revelation, to a period of **one hour** associated with trial or tribulation?'

The answer is: 'Yes'.

> '... *the ten horns which you saw are ten kings who have received no kingdoms as yet, but they receive authority for* **one hour** *as kings with the beast.'*   (Revelation 17:12)

> '*These are of one mind, and they will give their power and authority to the beast.'*   (Revelation 17:13)

Authority was given for 'one hour' as kings with the beast.

Is there any further reference elsewhere in Revelation that mentions this authority and connects it to a period of time, which the phrase one hour could refer to?

The answer is: 'Yes'.

> '*And he* (the beast) *was given a mouth speaking great things and blasphemies, and he was given authority to continue for forty-two months.'*   (Revelation 13:5)

We believe therefore that we can reasonably deduce that the hour of trial that Jesus warns of in his letter to the Philadelphians, in all probability, also foreshadows, or typifies the Great tribulation referred to in Daniel 12:7, as *'time, times and half a time'*, i.e. three-and-a-half years or forty-two months.

> **Therefore, 'one hour' = 'forty two months' = 'the hour of trial', or the Great tribulation.**

Some Pre-/Mid-tribulationists believe that the use of the phrase 'kept from the hour', refers to the hour of tribulation or the forty-two months and that the 'open door' must therefore be the same 'door' John describes in Revelation 4:1. Proof indeed that the church **must** be raptured before the tribulation begins! They offer further evidence for a case for a Pre-tribulation rapture of the saints – referring to Jesus words:

> *'And as it was in the days of Noah, so it will be also in the days of the Son of Man: They ate, they drank they married wives, they were given in marriage, until the day that Noah entered the ark, and the flood came and destroyed them all. Likewise as it was also in the days of Lot: They ate, they drank, they bought, they sold, they planted they built; but on the day that Lot went out of Sodom it rained fire and brimstone from heaven and destroyed them all. Even so will it be in the day when the Son of Man is revealed.'*
>
> (Luke 17:26–30)

The first two illustrations are examples of how God waited until Noah and Lot were safely out of harm's way, before bringing sudden destruction upon the earth in Noah's case and upon the city of Sodom in the case of Lot.

The third illustration is prophetic and here Jesus promises deliverance for the saints before God's wrath is poured out on the earth. But the deliverance is from God's **wrath** and the two examples Jesus gives, denote deliverance followed by **sudden destruction** – not a period of tribulation. Furthermore Jesus promises this deliverance *'in the day when the Son of Man is* **revealed***'* – *not in a secret rapture!*

The Derby/Scofield – Dispensational View

Placing 'Peter's Time Formula' to one side, the Dispensational Pre-tribulation view is that the Body of Christ will not have to go through the tribulation. The Saints will be taken up to heaven for seven years. Israel and the rest of the world will face the tribulation and the wrath of God. During this period great multitudes will be saved and many will be martyred, both Jews and Gentiles.

But are those surviving Jews and Gentiles having heard the gospel and received Jesus amidst the desperate days of the tribulation, to discover that the promises of the Lord do not fully apply to them, because they were apparently saved at the 'wrong time'? Too late for the Rapture and too late for the Wedding?

This Pre-tribulation view holds that **only** the raptured Church is the Bride of Christ and that these 'tribulation saints', both Jew and Gentile are not included, because the church and Israel have their own **separate eternal** destinies.

If all this is true, then what about the following scriptures? The Authorised New King James Bible states:

> *'For we being many are one bread, and one body: for we are all partakers of that one bread.'* (1 Corinthians 10:17)

> *'For as the body is one and has many members, but all the members of that one body, being many, are one body, so also is the Christ. For by one Spirit we were all baptized into one body – whether Jews or Greeks, whether slaves or free – and have all been made to drink into one Spirit.'*
> (1 Corinthians 12:12–13)

and Paul, himself a Jew, writes in Romans 11:23:

> *'And they also* (the natural branches, the Jews), *if they do not continue in unbelief, will be grafted in, for God is able to graft them in again.'*

The Scripture speaks of branches (plural) and one olive tree (singular). Surely natural branches which have been broken off and grafted into (their own) olive tree again, share a common eternal destiny with the grafted in un-natural branches?

> *' "Come I will show you the Lamb's wife." And he carried me away in the Spirit to a great and high mountain, and showed me the great city, the holy Jerusalem, descending out of heaven from God ... Also she had a great and high wall with twelve gates, and twelve angels at the gates, and names written on them, which are the names of the twelve tribes of the children of Israel: ... Now the wall of the city had*

twelve foundations, and on them were the names of the twelve apostles of the Lamb.' (Revelation 21:9, 10, 12, 14)

Here John refers to the holy city, the New Jerusalem, the common destiny of all believers including the Jewish elect. Thus the Pre-tribulation view that maintains Israel and the Church have **different and separate** eternal futures is not borne out by these scriptures. If Jesus is in eternity with the Church, how can he also be in eternity with Israel, unless the two are **together**?

Are there **two** eternities, **two** flocks, **two** shepherds?

Jesus Himself says,

*'And other sheep I have which are not of this fold; them also I must bring, and they will hear My voice; and there will be **one** flock and **one** shepherd.'* (John 10:16)

The Marriage of the Lamb

We believe the key to the Pre-/Post-tribulation rapture debate hinges on our correct interpretation and understanding of the Marriage of the Lamb as described in Revelation 19:7:

'...and His wife has made herself ready.'

If this literal assembling of **all** the saints/elect (his wife) **including** the tribulation saints **and** the Jewish remnant can be explained, then everything else concerning the Rapture/ Second Coming, will fall into place!

The view that claims that Israel and the Church have separate eternal destinies can be shown to be mistaken. Much has been made of the fact that the first three chapters of Revelation refer almost exclusively to the Church. The Pre-tribulationists therefore conclude that, 'the Church must be raptured **before** the tribulation, because the word "**Church**" is not mentioned in the descriptions of the tribulation on earth in Revelation chapters 4–19'! But the word 'church' is not mentioned in the description of the New Heaven and

Earth either; but rest assured – the Saints will most certainly be there!

We believe the answer as to why the 'Church' is not mentioned in Revelation 4–19 is very simple:

The first part of John's vision places him on the Isle of Patmos. Jesus appears to him there and instructs him to,

> 'Write the things which you have seen (the vision of Christ), and the things which are (the seven angels and the seven churches), and the things which will take place after this.' (Revelation 1:19)

The visions contained in Revelation chapters 2 and 3 then follow.

Pre-tribulational Rapture Doctrine

The Great Tribulation:
Rapture: Second Coming: Millenium: Eternity

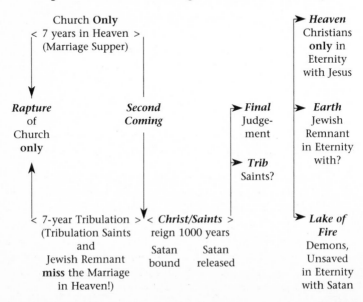

Post-tribulation Rapture – according to Peter's Time Formula

The Great Tribulation:
Rapture/Second Coming: Millenium: Eternity

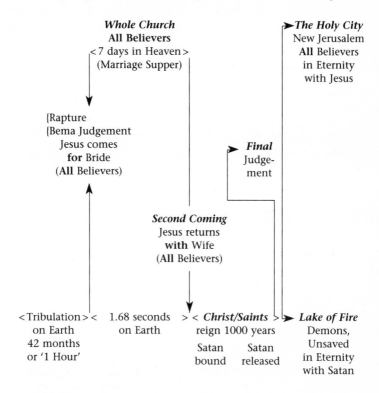

The scene then moves from the earth (where the seven churches are depicted) to heaven. John says in Revelation 4:1–2:

> *'After these things* (the references to the vision of the churches **on earth**) *I looked, and behold, a door standing open in heaven. And the first voice which I heard was like a trumpet speaking with me, saying, "Come up here, and I will show you things which must take place after this." Immediately I was in the Spirit; and behold, a throne set in heaven, and One who sat on the throne.'*

Note that John in his vision, has now left the earth (**the seven churches remaining behind on it!**) and is now seeing 'things which must take place after this' from heaven's perspective!

That there is no mention of the church in Revelation between chapters 4 and 19 is quite simply because the church is not yet present in heaven where John is, but still **on the earth**!

The church does not appear in heaven, until its presence is required, for two reasons:

1.   To be spared the Wrath of God poured out by the seventh angel from the seventh vial at the sound of the seventh trumpet! (Revelation 11:15 and 16:15–16).
2.   To be married to the Lamb! (Revelation 19:7).

We have described what we believe the Lord showed us as to **how** the Rapture of **all** the Saints will happen.

We now describe what we believe the Lord showed us as to **when** this will happen!

Chapter 23

The Rapture of the Saints and the Second Coming of the Lord Jesus Christ

by Malcolm

Immediately after the tribulation of those days when the sun will be darkened and the moon will not give its light, there will come a moment in time, pre-determined by God the Father, when the Lord Jesus Christ will descend from Heaven.

> *'Behold, I am coming as a thief. Blessed is he who watches, and keeps his garments, lest he walk naked and they see his shame.'* (Revelation 16:15)

The dead in Christ, followed by the living believers, will be instantaneously raised, **'Out of Darkness into His Marvellous Light'**, to meet Him in the air to appear before the Bema Judgement seat.

> *'For the Lord Himself will descend from heaven with a shout, with the voice of an archangel, and with the trumpet of God. And the dead in Christ will rise first. Then we who are alive and remain shall be caught up together with them in the clouds to meet the Lord in the air. And thus we shall always be with the Lord.'* (1 Thessalonians 4:16, 17)

'And behold, I am coming quickly, and My reward is with Me, to give to every one according to his work.'

(Revelation 22:12)

The rewarded, glorified Saints will then be instantaneously transported to heaven, where the Marriage Supper of the Lamb and His Bride, will take place. This entire glorious series of events including the seven day Wedding Feast in heaven, will take no more than **1.68** seconds of earth time! At the conclusion of the Marriage Supper, the glorified Saints (now His Wife), will then follow the Lord out of heaven (Revelation 19:14), and arrive back on earth, with a little over a second and a half having elapsed on earth!

The apostle Paul wrote:

*'Behold, I tell you a mystery: We shall not all sleep, but we shall all be changed – in a moment, in the twinkling of an eye, **at the last trumpet**. For the trumpet shall sound, and the dead shall be raised incorruptible, and we shall be changed.'*   (1 Corinthians 15:51–52)

The *Oxford English Dictionary* defines 'twinkling' as, 'of eyelids and eyes, to close and open', in other words to blink. The average time it takes to blink an eye, is one tenth of one second. Imagine a person, standing on the earth watching a living believer at the very instant of the rapture. They would only have to **blink** and they would miss it! The believer would have disappeared in front of their very eyes!

In a further 1.58 seconds that believer would have been raptured; received their glorified body and reward; taken instantly to Heaven; married to the Lamb as part of the Bride; celebrated for seven days at the Wedding Feast; and returned to the earth with the Lord, as part of His Wife.

'For as the lightning comes from the east and flashes to the west, so also will the coming of the Son of Man be.'

(Matthew 24:27)

Imagine again if you will, that same person, seeing the believer disappear in front of his very eyes, and in a little over a second and a half later, being almost blinded by a tremendous lightning flash in the sky. Suddenly, there upon the clouds, for all the world to see, will be the **Apokolupsis** (Greek: Revelation) of the Lord Jesus Christ, with power and great glory, together with the millions of His saints and countless angels.

> *'Wherever the body is, there the eagles will be gathered together.'* (Luke 17:37)

> *'...those who wait on the L*ORD
> *Shall renew their strength;*
> *They shall mount up with wings like eagles.'*
> (Isaiah 40:31)

All the horrors of the Tribulation will be as nothing, compared to the fear and terror that will seize the hearts of those that dwell on the earth on that 'great and terrible' day.

When will the Rapture occur? Paul tells us **exactly** when the Rapture will occur in 1 Corinthians 15:51–52 – **'at the last trumpet.'**

The Last Trumpet Means – the Last Trumpet!

> *'Behold, I tell you a mystery: We shall not all sleep, but we shall all be changed – in a moment, in the twinkling of an eye, **at the last trumpet**. For the trumpet will sound, and the dead will be raised incorruptible, and we shall be changed.'*

We believe it is the **same** trumpet described in 1 Thessalonians 4:16–17 – the 'rapture' scripture:

> *'For the Lord Himself will descend from heaven with a shout, with the voice of an archangel, and with the trumpet of God. And the dead in Christ will rise first. Then we who are alive and remain shall be caught up together with them in the clouds to meet the Lord in the air. And thus we shall always be with the Lord.'*

And the **same** trumpet described in:

> *'Then the sign of the Son of Man will appear in heaven, and
> then all the tribes of the earth will mourn, and they will see
> the Son of Man coming on the clouds of heaven with power
> and great glory. And He will send His angels with a great
> sound of a trumpet, and they will gather together His elect
> from the four winds, from one end of heaven to the other.'*
>
> (Matthew 24:30–31)

And the **same** trumpet described in:

> *'Then the seventh angel sounded . . . '*   (Revelation 11:15)

'The last trump', 'the trumpet of God', 'a great sound of a
trumpet, and the trumpet 'sounded by the seventh angel',
described in these scriptures we believe to be **one and the
same**.

We believe these scriptures all refer to the last trumpet,
the very last trumpet of the Revelation series of seven
and the very last trumpet mentioned in the Bible. We have
searched the scriptures and can find no reference to any
further trumpets sounding, after this one, so the last
trumpet of Revelation 11:15 **must** be the same trumpet Paul
refers to as 'the last trump'.

If this is the case, then this is indeed the trumpet that
signals the rapture of the Church and virtually simultaneously, the second advent, as we have described.

'Peter's Time Formula' is the key here, which unlocks the
mystery of how this could be possible. The last of the seven
vials is poured out as this final trumpet sounds. This vial
contains 'the cup of the wine of the fierceness of God's
wrath.' As it is poured out a great voice from the throne of
heaven says, **'It is done.'**

The last gigantic earthquake of all time then rocks the
entire planet (see Appendix D): cities around the world
collapse; islands and mountains simply disappear; enormous
hailstones weighing 120 lbs, fall upon the earth.

These descriptions of terrible destruction are 'cross-
referenced' (Revelation 16:17–21; 11:19 and 6:12–17), where

they all describe the same event, the final outpouring of God's wrath upon those who dwell on earth.

In the literal split second, immediately preceding this outpouring, Jesus returns for, and leaves the earth, with His Bride.

> *'Behold, I am coming as a thief. Blessed is he who watches and keeps his garments, lest he walk naked and they see his shame.'* (Revelation 16:15)

This is the very moment of the Rapture described by Paul in 1 Thessalonians 4:15–17; 5:2 and 2 Thessalonians 2:2.

The Rapture is also cross-referenced in Revelation 11:18, immediately before the description of God's final wrath (Revelation 19). Paul states:

> *'For God did not appoint us to wrath, but to obtain salvation through our Lord Jesus Christ.'* (1 Thessalonians 5:9)

The dead and alive in Christ will not experience this wrath, but instead they will be caught up – and ever be with the Lord. **Peter's Time Formula** is the only explanation that allows that vital space in time, however brief, between the Rapture and the Second Coming for **all** the saints/elect, both living and dead to stand before the Bema Judgement seat, become the Wife of Christ, including time for the Marriage Supper in heaven, and arrive back on earth with Him for His Second Coming. Sceptics may say that the outpouring of God's wrath will still be taking place as they arrive back 1.68 seconds later! This may be true, but when they return with the Lord, the saints will be in glorified bodies and indestructible as He is indestructible and will not thus be subject to God's wrath. In fact Revelation 19:15 says of Jesus when He returns with the saints:

> *'...**He Himself** treads the winepress of the fierceness and wrath of Almighty God.'*

It is clear from the Book of Revelation that during the great tribulation, many of the saints will be persecuted and killed – so will any survive?

What about Jesus' promise to the faithful saints that they will be *'kept from the Hour'* (the Great tribulation)?

The other promises to the 'faithful' church in Revelation 3, include:

> *'See I have set before you an open door...'*
>
> *'I also will keep you from the hour of trial which shall come upon the whole world, to test those who dwell on earth.'*

The phrase, *'those who dwell on earth'*, is used to describe mankind in opposition to God (Revelation 6:10; 8:13; 11:10; 13:3, 8, 12, 14; 14:3, 6; 17:2, 8).

Jesus indeed promises to keep the **'faithful'** church (a 'type' of true believers) from *'the hour of trial'* (Revelation 3:10) (which we believe refers to the Great tribulation of forty-two months).

As already stated the Pre-tribulation view is that this promise is fulfilled in the rapture of the church before the trouble begins on earth.

But in His letters to the seven churches, it is **only** the faithful church, with which Jesus found no fault, that receives His promise of divine protection.

Why?

> *'I know your works ... you ... have kept My word, and have not denied My name ... because you have kept My command to persevere.'*   (Revelation 3:8–10)

The original faithful church in Philadelphia was active in keeping the Lord's word; did not disavow Him; and did faithfully utter, tell, share with others, preach the Gospel, whilst hopefully enduring with patience. This description is of a group of **pro-active**, rather than **passive**, believers. This is the opposite of the 'falling away' (Greek: *'apostasia'*), described in 2 Thessalonians 2:3 when many believers will, 'stand away from or distance themselves' from the faith and from the Lord, because of fear of persecution.

This scenario is therefore descriptive of a time when the church will be under great pressure, *'for you have a little strength'* (Revelation 3:8), when believers will experience, trials and persecution for their faith. This hardly fits the description of the condition of most believers today at least in the Western World, who at the moment do not face persecution and have a relatively peaceful life. Yet Pre-tribulationsts in their doctrine of 'Imminency', tell us that we can be raptured at any time! If Revelation 3:10 is interpreted literally, as it reads, then it shows a church remaining faithful in the midst of trouble and tribulation, yet still fearlessly proclaiming the Gospel whilst enduring patiently, waiting for their deliverance.

So under these circumstances how can the rapture be **Pre**-tribulational?

The Great Tribulation is Not the Wrath of God!

Paul tells us that we are not appointed to wrath. So if the *'kept from the hour'* promise of Jesus does not extend to the **other** six churches, which despite their spiritual condition, if they repent, are nevertheless still part of the body of Christ – then Jesus could **not** possibly have been referring here to God's wrath, from which **every** believer will be 'kept'.

We must therefore conclude that the 'hour' that Jesus was referring to, cannot be the wrath of God, but the **forty-two months of tribulation** in the time of the end.

- He promises that only the **faithful** church will be kept from the hour of trial.
- He does not describe how He will do it!
- We believe we have shown it cannot be by Pre-tribulation Rapture.
- We do not think that the method matters.
- He has promised to do it. His word is enough!
- Our Faith must meet His Grace.

There is however a condition attached to His promise to the faithful church.

Chapter 24

Can Believers Survive the Tribulation? The Open Door and the Hour of Trial

by Malcolm

'See, I have set before you an open door, and no one can shut it; for you have a little strength, have kept My word, and have not denied My name.' (Revelation 3:8)

T his 'open door' is not a 'heavenly' door through which the whole church escapes to heaven in a secret rapture, prior to the tribulation, for as we have seen, Jesus does not set this open door before any of the other six churches. It is the same door Paul describes in 1 Corinthians 16:9 and 2 Corinthians 2:12, as the door of **evangelistic** opportunity or service.

All those believers then, who would desire the Lord to keep them from the 'hour of trial', i.e. preserve them through the Great tribulation, are to carry out faithfully the Lord's Great Commission:

*'... Go into all the world and **preach the gospel** to every creature. He who believes and is baptised will be saved; but he who does not believe will be condemned. And these signs will follow those who believe: In My name they will cast out demons; they will speak with new tongues; they will take up serpents; and if they drink anything deadly, it will by no*

> *means hurt them; they will lay hands on the sick, and they*
> *will recover.'* (Mark 16:15–18)

If He supernaturally preserves those faithful evangelistic believers, whether many or few in number, along with the sealed 144,000 of Israel, through the tribulation on earth, so that together, they may be the only believers left alive at the rapture, then He has kept his promise!

Acts Chapter 8

> *'...a great persecution arose against the church which was*
> *at Jerusalem; and they were all scattered throughout the*
> *regions of Judea and Samaria ... As for Saul, he made havoc*
> *of the church, entering every house, and dragging off men*
> *and women, committing them to prison.* **Therefore** *those*
> *who were scattered went everywhere* **preaching the word.'**

Note the use of the word, *'therefore'*.

Does it make any sense that people who were under severe threat of imprisonment and death, who were scattered and driven from their homes, should go everywhere **preaching** the very word that brought them persecution?

Does it make any sense, that many of those who heard the word and knew that it would undoubtedly also bring them persecution too, nevertheless, repented and sought forgiveness of sin and gladly accepted salvation through Jesus of Nazareth who had recently been crucified for 'blasphemy'?

Of course not. It makes no sense at all to the natural man. But perfect sense to God.

Jesus' answer to Satan's Great tribulation is – *His Great Commission*!

In Revelation 14:6 John sees,

> *'...another angel flying in the midst of heaven, having the*
> *everlasting gospel to preach to those who dwell on the earth –*
> *to every nation, tribe, tongue, and people...'*

Margaret and I believe it is these ones who are described as the faithful church that will be preaching the gospel at this time to those who dwell on earth.

We believe the debate on the question of a Pre-tribulation, Mid-tribulation or a Post-tribulation Rapture can now be resolved. The differing views have their answer in a mighty move of God that will snatch from the earth the completed mystery of God, the Body of Christ, His Bride, both the living and the dead in the Lord and translate them to heaven for the Marriage Supper. This will occur some time after the tribulation, in a split second, just before God's Holy wrath is poured out on the earth. Virtually simultaneously with the Rapture will be the Return of the Lord together with His Saints in Power and Glory. Because of the sense of tremendous speed that is involved in the Rapture and His Second Coming, Jesus is able to tarry, literally until almost the very last moment (even the last couple of seconds would be enough), until the Fullness of the Gentiles is completed. In this way His Father will send Him for His Bride and He will return to Earth, both **for** and **with**, the saints (Zechariah 14:5).

Thus the Great tribulation will be experienced not only by Israel and the rest of the World, but the **Church** as well. When Jesus and His saints arrive back on earth and He has destroyed the kings of the earth and their armies, those people who are left alive are those peoples and nations, who will populate the earth during the Millennium, to be ruled and reigned over by the Lord Jesus Christ and His Glorified Saints.

> ' . . . they shall be priests of God and of Christ, and shall reign with Him a thousand years.' (Revelation 20:6)

Some would argue that Jesus's ascension to Heaven in a cloud was a gradual event and that scripture says that He will return in the same manner. But it seems to us that initially at least, His ascension needed to be gradual in order to demonstrate to the disciples that He was indeed returning to His Father. At other times He appeared to the disciples, suddenly and without warning.

All the descriptions in scripture of the rapture and the second coming imply great rapidity, a miraculous event of amazing suddenness and speed. Many Christians have been taught that they will be raptured to heaven thus escaping the tribulation. Naturally, as we did, they take great comfort from this teaching. Many are trusting in the **rapture**, rather than in **Jesus**. We believe that the Bride of Christ needs to know this truth, unpopular as it will undoubtedly be.

There is not going to be any Pre- or Mid-tribulation 'escape' of the Church.

Is the Spirit Willing?

It is interesting at this point, to recall Jesus' words to His disciples in the garden of Gethsemane on the Eve of His crucifixion:

> *'Could you not watch with me for* **one hour***?'*

> *'The Spirit indeed is willing, but the flesh is weak.'*

In the last 'hour' Jesus promises His **special protection** for the 'Faithful Church'; together with the sealed and protected 144,000 Jews; i.e. those who will carry out His Great Commission.

Jesus said of the last hour:

> *'......he who endures to the end shall be saved. And this gospel of the kingdom will be preached in all the world as a witness to all nations, and then the end will come.'*
> (Matthew 24:13–14)

Who is to preach the Gospel to the world at this time if not the Church, Christ's Body on earth, distributed in all nations throughout the world?

Certainly not the 144,000 sealed Jews. How are they supposed to travel all over the world in the midst of disaster, war, earthquake etc.? If one cannot buy unless one has 'the mark of the beast' this would be difficult enough even without all the catastrophic events of Revelation going on. The 144,000 Jews are to spread the gospel of Jesus the Messiah in Israel, to their own people. Anyone who has been to Israel will know that with few exceptions, Jews will only listen to other Jews on matters of the Messiah; certainly not Christians.

The sealed Jews appointed task is to preach the Messiah and His Second Coming to a nation that will at last be ready to receive and believe the Word. The Holy Spirit will then remove the 'spiritual blindfold', that was placed over the Jewish minds, for the Gentiles sake.

We have discovered that many Christians are fearful of even thinking about the tribulation to come, preferring to hide their heads in the sand rather than holding their heads up, *'looking for their redemption to draw nigh.'* This is quite understandable, but if such Christians are afraid that Satan is going to have it all his own way, they are very much mistaken. Revelation describes disaster after disaster coming upon the earth. Wars, earthquakes, famine, fire, flood on a scale never before seen on earth.

Systematic persecution requires efficiency, planning, organisation and time. The early Christians were persecuted by the unopposed might of the highly organised Roman State. It is an entirely different matter to persecute and kill Christians when the world is falling down around your ears, when power lines are destroyed, when modern communication is constantly disrupted and computers refuse to function, when whole seas and rivers are poisoned, when wars are being fought with millions being killed. There will undoubtedly be great persecution of Christians to begin with, but we believe this will rapidly diminish as the persecutors worldwide concentrate on preserving their own skins!

The Nazi persecution of the Jews began in 1933, with the first concentration camps operating in 1938. They were able to carry out their 'final solution' initially because the so-called civilised countries of the world stood back and did nothing. However as the Allies later overran occupied Europe, it became increasingly difficult for the Germans to arrest and transport Jews from occupied Europe to the camps. In the final stages of the war, as Germany collapsed, the death machine broke down and the extermination process could not continue. Six million Jews perished. A terrible holocaust.

Even so, many Jews survived and went on to found the State of Israel in 1948.

Remember how God preserved the children of Israel through the plagues which fell on Egypt? The Egyptians died by the thousand from contaminated water and diseases caused by plagues of frogs, lice, flies, and dead livestock. Hail killed men in the fields, only in Goshen was there no hail. Locusts ate all the crops and vegetation, but only in Egypt. Thick darkness covered the land, but all the children of Israel had light in their dwellings. All the first born throughout the land died except those of the Israelites.

Isn't God the same yesterday, today and forever?

How much more will He care for His **faithful** Church on earth, carrying out His Great Commission. Undoubtedly some may fall in this cause. None of us wants to be killed or martyred. But if a nation's soldiers are prepared to go to war and perhaps even be killed on behalf of a mere country, a piece of real estate, shouldn't we Christians also be prepared to make the supreme sacrifice if required, for the sake of the Gospel?

> *'And they overcame him by the blood of the Lamb and by the word of their testimony, and they did not love their lives to the death.'* (Revelation 12:11)

What is the worst that can happen to a believer? Satan can take his life. But Jesus promises to give it back again, only better! Many millions of believers have died since Jesus was crucified, many were martyred, most died from natural causes. All over the world today, there are believers who are dying in car crashes, from cancer or worse, or are suffering lingering sickness and disease.

My father did not die a very pleasant death. He probably would have liked to have lived a few more years, even if those had to be tribulation years.

If we cannot buy or sell, because we will not accept the 'mark', so what? That's God's problem! God fed the Israelites for forty years in the desert, and neither their clothes nor shoes wore out! His pillar of cloud sheltered them from the sun by day, and His pillar of fire kept them warm by night.

During this period the Israelites too, could neither buy nor sell!

Our God is **well able** to preserve His faithful people through any tribulation.

It is those who dwell on earth, the unsaved who need to fear. It is those who do not know the Lord who are to be pitied. They are going to go through the tribulation just like the believers, only unlike the believers they have no eternal hope, no new life to come, no salvation through the shed blood of Jesus. Margaret and I believe that it is during this time of terrible tribulation that the multitudes who cannot be numbered will call on the name of the Lord and be eternally saved. For this reason the Church is **required** to be on earth! Who else is going to lead these ones to the Lord? The faithful witnessing believers will be like the Levites of old, in the vanguard, empowered as never before by the Holy Spirit, to heal the sick, drive out demons, cleanse the lepers, raise the dead and proclaim the imminent second coming of our Lord Jesus Christ! Margaret and I truly believe that God is even now pouring out His Spirit world-wide, preparing His people, anointing His chosen ones with great power, for the fast approaching day of His Second Coming.

David Pawson in his latest book, *Is the Blessing Biblical?* (p. 77, paragraph 2), states:

> 'The responsibility for preparing churches for tough times ahead is placed firmly on the churches them-selves (Revelation 2–3). Having said that, we cannot believe that the Lord would not play His part by strengthening them by His Spirit. It would be reason-able (though this is speculation) to expect a "move" of His Spirit to encourage the Church prior to a time of suffering.'

Maybe, but Margaret and I believe that the present pour-ing out of the Holy Spirit is not just to strengthen the Church in preparation for suffering and martyrdom, but to imbue His faithful Church with Holy Ghost Power!

Jesus promised that:

> *'Most assuredly, I say to you, he who believes in Me, the works that I do he will do also; and greater works than these he will do, because I go to My Father.'* (John 14:12)

Moreover Jesus continues:

> *'And whatsoever you ask in My name, that I will do, that the Father may be glorified in the Son. If you shall ask anything in My name, I will do it.'*

Has anyone done **greater** works than Jesus since He went to be with His Father?

The answer surely must be – No!

So was Jesus in error when He said those words?

Is He a man that He should lie? Of course not!

These greater works that Jesus spoke of must therefore take place **sometime**!

So, just **when** will believers do greater things than Jesus?

Margaret and I believe it will be during **the three-and-a-half years** of the Great Tribulation, a period of time which corresponds to the duration of Jesus' ministry on earth!

The faithful believers will at this time be imbued with such power of the Holy Spirit, the like of which will not have been seen since the creation of the world!

This seems to be confirmed in Daniel 11:32 which prophesies events during the time of Antiochus, foreshadowing the events of the Great Tribulation,

> *'Those who do wickedly against the covenant he shall corrupt with flattery; but the people who know their God shall be strong, and carry out **great exploits**.'*

Chapter 25

This is That!

by Malcolm

O n 19th June 1994 the Holy Spirit fell upon the Sunday morning meeting of the King's Church in a new and extraordinary manner. The previous week Derek Brown and the other pastors of the King's Church had attended a Rodney Howard Brown meeting in Birmingham and had fallen down under the power of the Spirit. On 19th June, along with the rest of the congregation, we knew something was different when waves of holy laughter swept through the body and Simon Yiend, a Pastor, crawled on his hands and knees to the front of the church and took the microphone. 'This is not funny,' spluttered Simon, 'It's serious,' was all he managed to say before he collapsed on the ground in fits of laughter. 'This is that,' said Derek, quoting Peter in Acts 'spoken of in the days of the prophet Joel.'

After that the church met every evening for many months; people laughed, shook, trembled, howled and wept as the Spirit fell upon them. Young men prophesied, old men described dreams, many people's lives were changed dramatically. On several occasions Margaret had to be practically carried out of the church, completely drunk in the Spirit, others were frozen motionless for hours at a time. I myself felt a heavy anointing of the Spirit which pinned me to my seat. I felt tremendous peace and at the same time great joy.

This was a manifestation of the Spirit which was completely new to the majority of Christians in the King's Church but that I had experienced before in January 1990, over four years previously. Several people in the church were alarmed and dismayed. A prominent member and lay preacher declared that this so-called move of the Spirit was nothing less than a deception. A great fuss broke out in the local newspapers as Spirit-filled Christians aired opposite views and opinions.

Many people looked only at the outward effect or human reactions to the Spirit's power and could not see that characters and patterns of behaviour were being transformed by the power of the Spirit in those persons who were yielded. Interestingly enough, I have not met a single person who has declared himself against this particular 'move of the Spirit' who has **actually** experienced it for themselves.

During the course of the following twelve months a number of people left the church and joined other churches where this move of the Spirit was less pronounced or completely absent. People talked about the 'Toronto Blessing' as though it had originated in that city.

Planeloads of Christians from all over the world made a sort of pilgrimage to Toronto in order to experience for themselves 'the blessing'. However, it all seems to have begun with Rodney Howard Brown at a meeting in The Carpenters Home Church in Lakeland, Florida in 1993. Rodney Howard Brown was invited to the King's Church in April 1995 to address those in leadership, including area overseers and pastoral house group leaders.

Margaret and I attended Rodney's meeting and were impressed with his authority, sincerity and simple Bible teaching. We were unexpectedly pressed into service as counsellors and found ourselves laying hands on and praying the infilling of the Spirit to many people, including pastors and ministers from other churches. All fell out under the power of the Spirit. The effect on some was dramatic, tears flowed and at least one new Christian fell on the floor speaking in tongues for the first time. Subsequently, Margaret and I were called upon by our pastor, Derek Brown, to lay hands and minister in the Spirit to many believers in the King's Church. It was at this time that we began to feel strongly that the Lord desired to use us in a healing capacity.

We began to receive prophetic 'words' and songs from the

Lord. We received a prophetic song from the Lord about marriages and that many couples in order to receive the 'new wine' should also seek to receive a new wine skin. One Sunday morning we were given permission from Derek our Pastor to minister specifically to married couples.

Because of our own previous experiences of marriage which had been disastrous to say the least, we felt that we were qualified in a small way to help people in this area, not from the viewpoint of counselling however, but by the laying on of hands and ministering the Spirit. Several couples told us subsequently that the Lord had shown them areas of their lives in their attitudes to each other that required healing and forgiveness and that their relationship had been strengthened and put on a new course as a result. We regularly prayed for the sick in church meetings at Derek's request and were thrilled to see several healings take place. These ranged from migraine attacks, arthritic conditions and sports injuries, to middle ear infections, asthmatic conditions and various pains and ailments.

One Sunday in June 1995, Margaret's brother-in-law Ken, who was visiting us with his wife, Mary, Margaret's sister, asked us to pray for him as next day he was due to visit hospital for further tests of a suspected prostate tumour. During a holiday in Lanzarote in January 1995 the Lord had clearly spoken to me regarding healing and the words that should be spoken over sickness and infirmity. I felt that the Lord had reminded me of Matthew 16:19 where Jesus said to Simon Peter:

> *'And I will give you the keys of the kingdom of heaven, and whatever you bind on earth will be bound in heaven, and whatever you loose on earth will be loosed in heaven.'*

Another prompt had come to Margaret from the Holy Spirit whilst watching an old war film on television. The word Bomber Command was on screen and the Lord quickened **'command'** and impressed on her that she should use that word in speaking wholeness to people who were sick. Christians have the authority, it has been given to us by Jesus, and we need to use it.

So in faith we laid hands on Ken and declared the following:

> 'We take authority over all the works of the enemy in your body and we bind them in the mighty name of Jesus Christ, we loose the power of your Holy Spirit Lord, into Ken's body and we command this tumour to be destroyed in Jesus' name. We command this prostate to function normally as you intended. We thank you Lord for Ken's healing in the name of Jesus. Amen.'

We were delighted to learn several weeks later that the prostate-specific antigen blood test used to diagnose potential prostate cancers showed that the count had fallen from a very high level to a level which indicated that the tumour had disappeared completely. We gave thanks and praise and glory to the Lord.

In June 1995, our pastor, Derek prophesied over a number of people. Derek prophesied over Margaret and me:

> 'With humility, receive the word that is able to save your soul. Don't just rely on gift or togetherness or anointing – the test is My Word. You see people need faith and that comes from you, because you have an anointing but they need faith to receive that anointing, and that too will be imparted to them from you. You need to put faith in the Word of God in a whole new way – not just words, but the Word of God. You're in a kind of wilderness place, just like Jesus when He knew that the power of the Spirit was coming, He knew the fullness of the Spirit, but He was able to say, "It is written." As you grow in the faith of God's Word you're going to release faith in others and that anointing will be a whole new measure of power in your life. A whole new level of power and anointing will be released to you. So put faith in My word, put faith in "It is written."'

Almost immediately in the following week, prior to praying for the sick, we began to receive many words of knowledge describing conditions and sicknesses which were afflicting people in the congregation. As we described what the Lord had given us many people came forward and as we laid hands on them and commanded their bodies to be healed in the name of Jesus, they went under the power of the Spirit. Many reported instant healings and others whose healing took place over a period of time. Some people were not healed at all. Frances Hunter has told us that the first four people she prayed for all died! We don't know why some people are healed, whilst others are not. We don't believe it is our responsibility to try and reason or work this out. God is sovereign and only He knows His reasons as to why He permits sickness in some and heals others.

Our duty is to carry out that part of the Lord's Great Commission – lay hands on the sick, in faith, expecting their healing and leave the rest to Him.

It was at this time, after giving my testimony at a small regional church meeting that I felt directed to write this testimony down. Bill Rice the Pastor at that meeting, prophesied that I would give my testimony in many places in front of many people.

Derek Brown had lent us a copy of *How to Heal the Sick* by Charles and Frances Hunter and when we discovered that they were coming to the UK in July 1995 we just knew that we had to enrol on their four-day training seminar. We drove to Manchester with Margaret's sister Mary and her husband Ken and spent the next four days in awe and admiration of the wonderful ministry that Charles and Frances Hunter have in the Lord. At the end of the four days we all went on the streets of Manchester and took part in one of the Hunter's 'Healing Explosions'!

Charles and Frances led the meeting in the central square and preached the Gospel. At the 'altar call' about eight people responded to Frances' appeal. She led them through the prayer of salvation and then immediately put them on the microphone to tell others what they had done! Charles and Frances were and are a tremendous inspiration to us and we will always remain grateful to them for their guidance and encouragement.

What was That?

Christians in many churches who were in the vanguard of this move of God's Spirit are apparently now asking, 'Where is the Revival that was prophesied?' What was it all about? People are reportedly disillusioned because of a seeming lack of response in non-believers to the outpouring of God's Spirit. Following on the heels of the seemingly disappointing outcome of such recent European Evangelistic initiatives such as, 'JIM' (Jesus In Me) and Reinhard Bonke's, 'Minus to Plus', this is understandable. Many charismatic leaders spoke of famous revivals in past years and believed that a great new revival that would sweep the land was imminent. People's expectations were raised and they were told to expect church growth that had not been seen since the Acts of the Apostles.

So What **was** That? What exactly was Joel describing in his prophecy?

A great in-gathering of sinners who turn to Jesus Christ at **the time of the end.**

This **end-time** 'revival' is described in Joel 2:28–32:

> '*And it shall come to pass afterward* (in the last days)
> *That I will pour out My Spirit on all flesh;*
> *Your sons and your daughters shall prophesy,*
> *Your old men shall dream dreams,*
> *Your young men shall see visions;*
> *And also on My menservants and on My maidservants*
> *I will pour out My Spirit in those days.*
> *And I will show wonders in the heavens and in the earth:*
> *Blood and fire and pillars of smoke.*
> *The sun shall be turned into darkness,*
> *And the moon into blood,*
> *Before the coming of the great and terrible day of the* LORD. ·
> *And it shall come to pass*
> *That whoever calls on the name of the* LORD
> *Shall be saved.*
> *For in Mount Zion and in Jerusalem there shall be*
>   *deliverance,*
> *As the* LORD *has said,*
> *Among the remnant whom the* LORD *calls.*'

Joel continues:

> 'Multitudes, multitudes in the valley of decision!
> For the day of the LORD is near in the valley of
>   decision.
> The sun and moon will grow dark,
> And the stars will diminish their brightness.'

(Joel 3:14–15)

It is obvious to anyone that although we may well have experienced elements of the first part of Joel's prophecy, the condition of the Sun and the Moon as they appear right now, are not as foreseen by Joel! Therefore the prophecy cannot be **fully** fulfilled until these conditions occur. This was so even in Peter's time at Pentecost.

So when exactly will these conditions occur and this prophecy be fulfilled?

What does God's word say?

> 'I looked when He opened the sixth seal, and behold, there was a great earthquake; and the sun became black as sackcloth of hair, and the moon became like blood.'

(Revelation 6:12)

> 'Then the fourth angel sounded: And a third of the sun was struck, a third of the moon, and a third of the stars, so that a third of them were darkened; and a third of the day did not shine, and likewise the night.'   (Revelation 8:12)

It is only at the time of the **Great Tribulation**, that the condition of the Sun and Moon are as foreseen by Joel occurs and multitudes, multitudes find themselves in the valley of decision.

> 'And I looked, and behold, a white cloud, and on the cloud sat One like the Son of Man, having on His head a golden crown, and in His hand a sharp sickle. And another angel came out of the temple, crying with a loud voice to Him who sat on the cloud, "Thrust in Your sickle and reap . . . for the

> *time of the harvest of the earth is ripe." So He who sat on the cloud thrust in His sickle and the earth was reaped.'*
>
> (Revelation 14:14–16)

As we have described, Margaret and I believe it will be in the midst of the Great Tribulation that the Holy Spirit will be poured out on faithful believers in the greatest measure **ever**. The world will witness the greatest revival since the foundation of the Church, when there will be widespread preaching of the Gospel, by the sealed 144,000 Jews in Israel and the faithful believers worldwide. Multitudes that cannot be counted will be saved, the earth will be reaped – then the end of the age will come.

(According to a recent BBC Radio News broadcast, a newly compiled DNA based survey of 350,000 Jewish priests, discovered that they all could be uniquely traced back, some 3,500 years, to a common ancestor, probably Aaron.)

So the 144,000 then, are already in place and at the right time will be sealed by God and will go forth to the rest of Israel preaching the Gospel of Salvation through the shed blood of Yeshua Hameshea!

We believe that this time is close at hand and that Joel's prophecy will soon be fulfilled in its entirety.

When the Bride of Christ realises this truth and purposes in faith to seek the Lord and trust in the power of His Holy Spirit in these last days, then the Spirit and the Bride will indeed, truly be ready to say,

> ' *"Come!" And let him who hears say, "Come!" And let him who thirsts come. And whoever desires, let him take the water of life freely.'*   (Revelation 22:17)

Chapter 26

Revelation Chapter Ten – The Capstone

by Malcolm

W hen we were in the USA in Summer 1995, during the meeting we referred to in Chapter 15, Mr Russell Bixler CEO of Cornerstone Television, prayed that God would give us further revelation on the subject of The Rapture of the Church and the Second Coming of the Lord. Sure enough when we were back in the UK several months after meeting Mr Bixler, when praying about this matter, Malcolm received a picture of a large stone block that was being lowered into place on the top of a large building together with the word, 'Capstone'. Now a capstone is the very last stone to be laid that completes a structure. The Spirit then led Malcolm to study Revelation 10. We believe the following to be the Capstone of the Mystery of God, and is further confirmation from scripture of the Post-tribulation rapture of the completed Church of Jesus Christ.

> *'And I saw still another mighty angel coming down from heaven, clothed with a cloud. And a rainbow was on his head, his face was like the sun, and his feet like pillars of fire. And he had a little book open in his hand. And he set his right foot on the sea and his left foot on the land, and cried with a loud voice, as when a lion roars. And when he cried out, seven thunders uttered their voices. Now when the seven thunders uttered their voices, I was about to write; but I heard a voice from heaven saying to me, "Seal up the things*

*which the seven thunders uttered, and do not write them."
And the angel whom I saw standing on the sea and on the
land lifted up his hand to heaven and swore by Him who
lives forever and ever, who created heaven and the things
that are in it, the earth and the things that are in it, and the
sea and the things that are in it, that there should be delay
no longer, but in the days of the sounding of the seventh
angel, when he is about to sound, the mystery of God would
be finished, as He declared to His servants the prophets.
Then the voice which I heard from heaven spoke to me again
and said, "Go, take the little book" ... And he said to me,
"Take and eat it; and it will make your stomach bitter, but it
will be as sweet as honey in your mouth." And I took the
little book out of the angel's hand and ate it, and it was as
sweet as honey in my mouth. But when I had eaten it, my
stomach became bitter. And he said to me, "You must
prophecy again about many peoples, nations, tongues, and
kings."'* (Revelation 10)

The mighty angel who John sees, has a unique combination of attributes and is described as:
1. Coming down from heaven.
2. Being clothed with a cloud.
3. Having a rainbow on his head.
4. Crying with a loud voice.
This angel further:
5. Swears that,

> *'there should be delay no longer, but in the days of the
> sounding of the seventh angel, when he is about to sound,
> the mystery of God would be finished, as He declared to
> His servants the prophets.'*

The mighty angel's actions are remarkably similar to those
described in 1 Thessalonians 4:16–17:

> *'For the Lord Himself will **descend from heaven** with a
> **shout**, with the **voice** of an **archangel**, and with the
> **trumpet** of God. And the dead in Christ will rise first. Then
> we who are alive and remain shall be caught up together*

*with them in the **clouds** to meet the Lord in the air. And*
thus we shall always be with the Lord.'

(We believe this angel to be Jesus himself. This seems to be
confirmed when later in Revelation 11:3 this angel says, *'And
I will give power to my two witnesses.'* Jesus is the only one
who can give power to those He refers to as **my** witnesses.)

The Mystery of God

The seventh angel is described in Revelation 11:15 and when
he begins to sound *'the seventh trumpet,'* is when the
*'**mystery** of God would be finished.'*

What is this **mystery** of God?

We believe this is the mystery referred to in Ephesians
3:1–7, 5:23–32; Colossians 1:26–29 and Romans 16:25–27.

Ephesians 3:1–7 states:

*'For this reason I, Paul, the prisoner of Jesus Christ for you
Gentiles – if indeed you have heard of the dispensation of the
grace of God which was given to me for you, how that by
revelation He made known to me the mystery (as I wrote
before in a few words, by which when you read, you may
understand my knowledge in the mystery of Christ), which in
other ages was not made known to the sons of men, as it has
now been revealed by the Spirit to His holy apostles and
prophets: that the Gentiles should be fellow heirs, of the
same body and partakers of His promise in Christ through
the gospel, of which I became a minister according to the gift
of the grace of God given to me by the effective working of
His power.'*

Ephesians 5:23–32 states:

*'For the husband is head of the wife, as also Christ is the
head of the church; and He is the Saviour of the body.
Therefore, just as the church is subject to Christ, so let the
wives be to their own husbands in everything. Husbands,
love your wives, just as Christ also loved the church and gave
Himself for it, that He might sanctify and cleanse it with the*

*washing of water by the word, that He might present it to Himself a glorious church, not having spot or wrinkle or any such thing, but that it should be holy and without blemish. So husbands ought to love their own wives as their own bodies; he who loves his wife loves himself. For no-one ever hated his own flesh, but nourishes and cherishes it, just as the Lord does the church. For we are members of His body, of His flesh and of His bones. "For this reason a man shall leave his father and mother and be joined to his wife, and the two shall become one flesh." This is a great **mystery**, but I speak concerning Christ and the church.'*

This mystery of God is described as being **finished** when the seventh angel **begins** to sound. The Greek word used here for 'finished' is *'teleo'* and in this context it means 'a completed work'. The Greek word for 'begins' is *'mello'* and is connected with expectation, i.e. 'to be about to do something (of persons or things – especially events)'.

It seems absolutely clear to us that the mystery that is being described in Revelation 10:7 is the completion of the Body of Christ or the Church – which will only be complete when the very last member or believer is added.

Pre-tribulationists have a very different interpretation of Revelation 10:7 and in his book, *Things to Come*, J.D. Pentecost writes:

'A necessary corollary of this argument is the interpretation of the mid-tribulationist that the mystery program of God that is finished (Revelation 10:7) is the mystery program of the church. The explanation of Ironside provides a better interpretation. He says:

"This is the theme of the seven-sealed roll; the vindication of God's holiness in having so long tolerated evil in His universe. What greater mystery confronts and confuses the human mind than the question, Why does God allow unrighteousness so often to triumph? ... This is His secret. He will disclose it in due time, and all shall be clear as the day ... His final triumph over all evil is what is so vividly presented in the rapidly shifting tableau of the Revelation. God is now terminating the program with evil." '

This explanation is a neat one but scripturally unsound! Scripture clearly shows that God's program with evil is **not** terminated until Satan is finally defeated at the end of the thousand-year reign of Jesus with the saints described in Revelation 20:10, when Satan is finally cast into the lake of fire.

Then, and only then, can it be said that God has terminated the program with evil.

A **finished** work of God is either a finished work of God or it is not! God does not half finish things or leave loose ends lying around.

We are convinced that the mystery that is described as being **finished** as the seventh angel begins to sound, is God's programme for the **Church**, i.e. **all** believers – the Body of Christ.

The rainbow on the head of the mighty angel signifies the covenant of grace that God established with Noah when he and his family were saved.

Noah and his family entered the Ark and then sudden destruction came upon the earth. When describing the 'rapture' of the church in 1 Thessalonians 4:16–17, Paul goes on to say in 1 Thessalonians 5:1–5:

> 'But concerning the times and seasons, brethren, you have no need that I should write to you. For you yourselves know perfectly that the day of the Lord so comes as a thief in the night. For when they say, "Peace and Safety!" then sudden destruction comes upon them, as labour pains upon a pregnant woman. And they shall not escape. But you, brethren, are not in darkness, so that this Day should overtake you as a thief. You are all sons of light and sons of the day. We are not of the night nor of darkness.'

In describing His second coming Jesus said:

> 'And as it was in the days of Noah ... Likewise as it was also in the days of Lot ... Even so will it be in the day when the Son of Man is revealed ... '

Sudden destruction came immediately **after** the Lord rescued both Noah and Lot!

It seems obvious to us that sudden destruction will follow the rapture of the completed church at the **last trump**, or the sounding of the **seventh trumpet** which we believe to be **one and the same**!

Sudden destruction does **not** follow, the rapture of the Church in the Pre-tribulation rapture theory, **tribulation** follows.

This tribulation, terrible as it undoubtedly will be – is **not** sudden destruction!

Sudden destruction is the completion of the wrath of God poured out on the earth, and believers have not been appointed to wrath. The sounding of the seventh trumpet coincides with the pouring out of the seventh and final bowl – God's completed wrath.

The body of Christ will not be complete and therefore cannot be taken up to heaven **until** the very last believer is added to the body.

This completion is described as not being complete or finished **until** the seventh trumpet **begins** to be sounded.

Nothing could be clearer.

This agrees exactly with Paul's description of believers being changed, *'at the last trump'*!

The Pre-tribulation theory acknowledges that the Church **cannot** possibly be raptured **until** this programme is completed.

J.D. Pentecost, again from his book, *Things to Come*, states:

> 'The partial rapturist must deny the New Testament teaching on the unity of the body of Christ. According to 1 Corinthians 12:12–13, all believers are united to the body of which Christ is the Head (Ephesians 5:30). This baptising experience is true of every regenerated individual. If the rapture includes only a portion of those redeemed, then the body, of which Christ is the head, will be a dismembered and disfigured body when it is taken to Him. The building, of which He is the chief cornerstone, will be incomplete.

The priesthood, of which He is the High Priest, will be without a portion of its complement. The Bride, in relation to whom He is the Bridegroom, will be disfigured. The new creation, of which He is the Head, will be incomplete. Such is impossible to imagine.'

On this J.D. Pentecost and ourselves are in agreement, scripture is very clear on this, the Lord returns just once – and He returns for **all** the believers! His body! The Church! There is no scriptural evidence of an 'advance party' or a portion of believers being caught up first. There is no evidence of the Lord coming back again for 'stragglers'.

We have to face the facts – the body of Christ is going **nowhere** until the very last believer has been added and the Bride is complete.

According to scripture that will not happen until the last trumpet begins to sound and the Lord returns for His Bride – *'after the tribulation of those days'!*

Chapter 27

Things to Come?
by Malcolm

I n 1961 the great American Evangelist, Tommy Hicks, gave the following prophecy:

Vision of the Body of Christ and the End-time Ministries

'My message begins July 25, about 2.30 in the morning at Winnipeg, Canada. I had hardly fallen asleep when the vision and the revelation that God gave me came before me. The vision came three times, exactly in detail, the morning of July 25, 1961. I was so stirred and so moved by the revelation that this has changed my complete outlook upon the body of Christ, and upon the end-time ministries. The greatest thing that the church of Jesus Christ has ever been given lies straight ahead. It is so hard to help men and women to realise and understand the thing that God is trying to give to his people in the end times.

I received a letter several weeks ago from one of our native evangelists down in Africa, down in Nairobi. This man and his wife were on their way to Tanganyika. They could neither read nor could they write, but we had been supporting them for over two years. As they entered into the territory of Tanganyika, they came across a small village. The entire village was evacuating because of a plague that had hit the village. He came across natives that were weeping, and he asked them what was wrong. They told him of their mother and father who had suddenly died, and they had been dead for three days. They had to leave. They were afraid to go in; they were leaving them in the cottage. He turned and asked them where they were. They pointed to the hut and he asked them to go with him, but they refused. They were afraid to go. The native and his wife went to this little cottage and entered in where the man and woman had been dead for three days. He simply stretched forth his hand in the name of the Lord Jesus Christ, and spoke the man's name and the woman's name and said, "In the name of the Lord Jesus Christ, I command life to come back to your bodies."

Instantaneously these two heathen people who had never known Jesus Christ as their Saviour sat up and immediately began to praise God. The Spirit and the power of God came into the life of those people.

To us that may seem strange and a phenomenon, but that is the beginning of these end-time ministries. God is going to take the do-nothings, the nobodies, the unheard-of, the no-accounts. He is going to take every man and every woman and he is going to give them this outpouring of the Spirit of God.

In the book of Acts we read that **"In the last days,"** *God said,* **"I will pour out my Spirit upon all flesh."** *I wonder if we realised what he meant when God said,* **"I will pour out my Spirit upon all flesh."** *I do not think I fully realise nor could I understand the fullness of it, and then I read from the book of Joel:*

> **"Be glad then, ye children of Zion, and rejoice in the Lord your God: for he hath given you the former rain moderately, and he will cause to come down for you the rain, the former rain, and the latter rain ... "**
>
> *(Joel 2:23)*

It is not only going to be the rain, the former rain and the latter rain, but he is going to give to his people in these last days a double portion of the power of God!

As the vision appeared to me after I was asleep, I suddenly found myself in a great high distance. Where I was, I do not know. But I was looking down upon the earth. Suddenly the whole earth came into my view. Every nation, every kindred, every tongue came before my sight from the east and the west, the north and the south. I recognised every country and many cities that I had been in, and I was almost in fear and trembling as I beheld the great sight before me: and at that moment when the world came into view, it began to lightning and thunder.

As the lightning flashed over the face of the earth, my eyes went downward and I was facing the north. Suddenly I beheld what looked like a great giant, and as I stared and looked at it, I was almost bewildered by the sight. It was so gigantic and so great. His feet seemed to reach to the north pole and his head to the south. Its arms were stretched from sea to sea. I could not even begin to understand whether this be a mountain or this be a giant, but as I watched, I suddenly beheld a great giant. I could see his head was struggling for life.

He wanted to live, but his body was covered with debris from head to foot, and at times this great giant would move his body and act as though it would even raise up at times. And when it did, thousands of little creatures seemed to run away. Hideous creatures would run away from this giant, and when he would become calm, they would come back.

All of a sudden this great giant lifted his hand toward the heaven, and then it lifted its other hand, and when it did, these creatures by the thousands seemed to flee away from this giant and go into the darkness of the night. Slowly this great giant began to rise and as he did, his head and hands went into the clouds. As he rose to his feet he seemed to have cleansed himself from the debris and filth that was upon him, and he began to raise his hands into the heavens as though praising the Lord, and as he raised his hands, they went even unto the clouds.

Suddenly, every cloud became silver, the most beautiful silver I have ever known.

As I watched this phenomenon it was so great I could not even begin to understand what it all meant.

I was so stirred as I watched it, and I cried unto the Lord and I said, "Oh, Lord, what is the meaning of this," and I felt as if I was actually in the Spirit and I could feel the presence of the Lord even as I was asleep.

And from those clouds suddenly there came great drops of liquid light raining down upon this mighty giant, and slowly, slowly, this giant began to melt, began to sink itself in the very earth itself, and as he melted, his whole form seemed to have melted upon the face of the earth, and this great rain began to come down. Liquid drops of light began to flood the very earth itself and as I watched this giant that seemed to melt, suddenly it became millions of people over the face of the earth. As I beheld the sight before me, people stood up all over the world! They were lifting their hands and they were praising the Lord.

At that very moment there came a great thunder that seemed to roar from the heavens. I turned my eyes toward the heavens and suddenly I saw a figure in white, in glistening white – the most glorious thing that I have ever seen in my entire life. I did not see the face, but somehow I knew it was the Lord Jesus Christ, and he stretched forth his hand, and as he did, he would stretch it forth to one, and to another, and to another . . .

And as he stretched forth his hand upon the nations and the people of the world – men and women – as he pointed toward them, this liquid light seemed to flow from his hands into them, and a mighty anointing of God came upon them, and those people began to go forth in the name of the Lord.

I do not know how long I watched it. It seemed it went into days and weeks and months. And I beheld this Christ as he continued to stretch forth his hand; but there was a tragedy. There were many people as he stretched forth his hand that refused the anointing of God and the call of God. I saw men and women that I knew. People that I felt would certainly receive the call of God. But as he stretched forth his hand toward this one and toward that one, they simply bowed their head and began to back away. And each of those that seemed to bow down and back away, seemed to go into darkness. Blackness seemed to swallow them everywhere.

I was bewildered as I watched it, but these people that he had anointed, hundreds of thousands of people all over the world, in Africa, England, Russia, China, America, all over the world, the anointing of God was upon these people as they went forward in the name of the Lord. I saw these men and women as they went forth. They were ditch diggers, they were washerwomen, they were rich men, they were poor men. I saw people who were bound with paralysis and sickness and blindness and deafness. As the Lord stretched forth to give them this anointing, they became well, they became healed, and they went forth!

And this is the miracle of it – this is the glorious miracle of it – those people would stretch forth their hands exactly as the Lord did, and it seemed as if there was this same liquid fire in their hands. As they stretched forth their hands they said, "According to my word, be thou made whole."

As these people continued in this mighty end-time ministry, I did not fully realise what it was, and I looked to the Lord and said, "What is the meaning of this?"

And he said, "This is that which I will do in the last days. I will restore all that the cankerworm, the palmerworm, the caterpillar – I will restore all that they have destroyed. This, my people, in the end times will go forth. As a mighty army shall they sweep over the face of the earth."

As I was at this great height, I could behold the whole world. I watched these people as they were going to and fro over the face of the earth.

Suddenly there was a man in Africa and in a moment he was transported by the Spirit of God, and perhaps he was in Russia, or China or America or some other place, and vice versa. All over the world these people went, and they came through fire, and through pestilence, and through famine. Neither fire nor persecution, nothing seemed to stop them. Angry mobs came to them with swords and with guns. And like Jesus, they passed through the multitudes and they could not find them, but they went forth in the name of the Lord, and everywhere they stretched forth their hands, the sick were healed, the blind eyes were opened. There was not a long prayer, and after I had reviewed the vision many times in my mind, and I thought about it many times, I realised that I never saw a church, and I never saw or heard a denomination, but these people were going in the name of the Lord of Hosts. Hallelujah! As they marched forth in everything they did as the ministry of Christ in the end times, these people were ministering to the multitudes over the face of the earth.

Tens of thousands, even millions seemed to come to the Lord Jesus Christ as these people stood forth and gave the message of the kingdom, of the coming kingdom, in this last hour. It was so glorious, but it seems as though there were those that rebelled, and they would become angry and they tried to attack those workers that were giving the message.

God is going to give to the world a demonstration in this last hour as the world has never known. These men and women are of all walks of life, degrees will mean nothing. I saw these workers as they were going over the face of the earth. When one would stumble and fall, another would come and pick him up. There were no "big I" and "little you", but every mountain was brought low and every valley was exalted, and they seemed to have one thing in common – there was a divine love, a divine love that seemed to flow forth from these people as they worked together, and as they lived together. It was the most glorious sight that I have ever known.

Jesus Christ was the theme of their life. They continued and it seemed the days went by as I stood and beheld this sight. I could only cry, and sometimes I laughed. It was so wonderful as these people went throughout the face of the whole earth, bringing forth in this last end time. As I watched from the very heaven itself, there were times when great deluges of this liquid light seemed to fall upon great congregations, and that congregation would lift their hands and seemingly praise God for hours and even days as the Spirit of God came upon them.

God said, **"I will pour my Spirit upon all flesh,"** and that is exactly this thing. And to every man and every woman that received this power, and the anointing of God, the miracles of God, there was no ending to it.

We have talked about miracles. We have talked about signs and wonders, but I could not help but weep as I read again this morning, at 4 o'clock this morning the letter from our native workers. This is only the evidence of the beginning for one man, a "do-nothing, and unheard-of", who would go and stretch forth his hand and say, "In the name of the Lord Jesus Christ, I command life to flow into your body." I *dropped to my knees and began to pray again, and I said, "Lord, I know that this thing is coming to pass, and I believe it's coming soon!"*

*And then again, as these people were going about the face of the earth, **a great persecution** seemed to come from every angle.*

Suddenly there was another great clap of thunder, that seemed to resound around the world, and I heard again the voice, the voice that seemed to speak, "Now this is my people. This is my beloved bride," and when the voice spoke, I looked upon the earth and I could see the lakes and the mountains.

The graves were opened and people from all over the world, the saints of all ages, seemed to be rising. And as they rose from the grave, suddenly all these people came from every direction. From the east and the west, from the north and the south, and they seemed to be forming again this gigantic body. As the dead in Christ seemed to be rising first, I could hardly comprehend it.

It was so marvellous. It was so far beyond anything I could ever dream or think of. But as this body suddenly began to form, and take shape again in the form of this mighty giant, but this time it was different.

It was arrayed in the most beautiful gorgeous white. Its garments were without spot or wrinkle as its body began to form and the people of all ages seemed to be gathered into this body, and slowly, slowly, as it began to form up into the very heavens, suddenly from the heavens above, the Lord Jesus came, and became the head, and I heard another clap of thunder that said, "This is my beloved bride for whom I have waited. She will come forth even tried by fire. This is she that I have loved from the beginning of time."

As I watched, my eyes suddenly turned to the far north, and I saw seemingly destruction: men and women in anguish and crying out, and buildings in destruction. Then I heard again, the fourth voice that said, "Now is My wrath being poured out upon the face of the earth."

From the ends of the whole world, the wrath of God seemed to be poured out and it seemed that there were great vials of God's wrath being poured out upon the face of the earth. I can remember it as though it happened a moment ago. I shook and trembled as I beheld the awful sight of seeing the cities, and whole nations going down into destruction. I could hear the weeping and wailing.

I could hear people crying. They seemed to cry as they went into caves, but the caves in the mountains opened up. They leaped into water, but the water would not drown them. There was nothing that could destroy them. They were wanting to take their lives, but they could not.

Then again I turned my eyes to this glorious sight, this body arrayed in beautiful white, shining garments. Slowly, slowly, it began to lift from the earth, and as it did, I awoke. What a sight I had beheld! I had seen the end-time ministries – the last hour. Again on July 27, at 2:30 in the morning, the same revelation, the same vision came again exactly as it had before.

My life has been changed as I realised that we are living in that end time, for all over the world God is anointing men and women with this ministry. It will not be doctrine. It will not be a churchianity. It is going to be Jesus Christ. They will give forth the word of the Lord, and are going to say, "I heard it so many times in the vision and according to my word it shall be done."

Oh, my people, listen to me. According to my word, it shall be done. We are going to be clothed with power and anointing from God. We won't have to preach sermons, we won't have to have persons heckle us in public. We won't have to depend on man, nor will we be denomination echoes, but we will have the power of the living God.

We will fear no man, but will go in the name of the Lord of Hosts!'

(Tommy Hicks' prophecy reproduced by kind permission of Charles and Frances Hunter.)

This wonderful End-Time prophecy of Tommy Hicks continues to thrill and excite Margaret and me. It seems to fit so closely what we believe the Lord has revealed to ourselves about the last hour (1260 days, forty-two months, three-and-a-half years). Note the similarities in the events and their order.

1. Ordinary believers willing to accept the Great Commission will be endued with great power.
2. Many will reject this commission – could this be the 'falling away'?
3. Great exploits, 'Signs and Wonders' – miracles will be done through the hands of these 'faithful' believers.
4. Nothing could stop them: neither fire, persecution, pestilence, famine, or attacks by angry mobs, they were 'kept from the hour of temptation'.
5. Multitudes – millions came to the Lord as these believers preached the Gospel in the last hour – to the ends of the earth.
6. A great persecution came upon them from every angle.
7. The graves were opened – the dead in Christ rose first – followed by these living saints. Jesus returned for His beloved Bride!
8. God's Wrath was poured out – sudden destruction came upon the earth.

Chapter 28

The Millennium and Beyond

by Malcolm

When we began to write this book, the Millennium seemed to us something of an enigma. As we understand it, the Millennium will be a thousand-year period of peace which begins with the return of the Lord, during which Satan will be bound and cast into the Abyss, placed out of circulation, unable to bring his influence on the world.

The Lord will have returned with His Saints who will be ruling and reigning with Him from the beloved city of Jerusalem. The Millennium will also be the interval between the first and second resurrections, the first being the resurrection of the righteous, ' the blessed and Holy'; i.e. those who are Christ's and the second resurrection, will take place at the end of the Millennium period on the day of judgement, for those who had rejected Christ and whose names were not in the Lamb's Book of Life and therefore were destined for the lake of fire. It is also the period when Israel will take its place at the head of all the nations of the world, when all God's covenant promises to the saved Jewish remnant will be fulfilled. Jerusalem will be the capital city of the world, from where Jesus will rule the planet with His Saints.

We could not readily see the reason why there should be a Millennium at all. If all those who were to have eternal life with the Lord in the new heaven and earth had their part in the first resurrection and over whom, 'the second death has no power', why bother with the Millennium? Why not proceed straight to judgement and the new heaven and earth?

We have read speculative theories that maintain that unbelieving Jews who survive the tribulation, will welcome Jesus' return to Jerusalem with rejoicing and celebration, realising that Jesus is the Messiah after all. However we cannot find any scripture which supports this rather wishful, but naive theory.

We believe that once Jesus returns to the earth with His Bride, the age of grace will be at an end. If there were further opportunity for salvation through faith in the Lord Jesus Christ **after** His return, then it would negate the trust of generations of believers, both Jew and Gentile who believed on the Lord, often ending their lives as martyrs for His sake.

It makes nonsense of the parable of the wise and foolish virgins. What would be the point of sending out 144,000 Gospel-preaching Jews to convert unbelievers prior to the return of Jesus, if someone who had rejected the message could simply change their mind when it suited them. What is the point of any believer following the Lord today, if he can have a second chance at some point in the future. What is the point of believers praying for loved ones to be saved? What is the point of preaching the Gospel and urging non-believers to make a decision for the Lord now, before it is **too late** if there is no such thing as too late?

What about all the people who have died through the generations, rejecting Jesus, even in death. If anyone has further opportunity for salvation **after** the Second Coming these people would have been treated unjustly. God is not unjust, He desires that all men should be saved, but He has given us all free will to decide for ourselves in an age of grace and that decision **must** be made either before an individual dies or before His Second Coming, when grace is ended. The Lord will return when the Fulness of the Gentiles is fulfilled and the Mystery of God is complete. The roll of the names in the Lamb's book of Life will be complete.

According to scripture, the wheat will be separated from the tares at the end of the age. David Pawson in his book, *The Return of Jesus* (p. 227–228), states that he believes that:

'the Millennium rule of Christ and His saints on this earth will be a visible vindication of Him and them in the eyes of the world ... the world (i.e. the unbelieving people on the earth, would otherwise never see the victory of good over evil.'

But why bother to demonstrate to unbelievers who are destined for the lake of fire anything at all?

In the days when there was capital punishment in this country the condemned man, after sentence had been passed was treated rather well, but there was no attempt to rehabilitate him or even castigate him further for his guilt. Once the sentence of death had been passed, that was the end of the matter as far as justice was concerned. It only remained for the sentence to be carried out. We cannot imagine that God could be teaching unbelievers, who are by definition, condemned and unredeemable any further lessons during this period – what benefit or value would it be to them in an eternal hell?

This would seem to be an unnecessary and rather vindictive act on God's part and out of character of the God of mercy and justice that we know. The lessons to be learned, we believe, are not for the condemned but for the redeemed of the Lord, His Saints. At the end of the thousand-year period, Satan is released once more to tempt the nations to rebel against Jesus and the Saints. Fire is sent down from heaven and the rebellious nations are defeated. Satan is cast into the lake of fire and brimstone. God's dealings with him are finally at an end. The old heavens and earth (presumably together with the space/time continuum) are consumed by fire and are no more.

Then comes the second resurrection and Judgement. All the unrighteous who have ever lived arise from the dead and receive resurrection bodies. Books are opened and these dead are judged according to their works. Anyone whose name is not found written in the Book of Life is cast into the lake of fire together with Death and Hades.

God then creates a new heaven and earth and reveals the holy city, New Jerusalem which is where God will dwell with the Saints, for evermore. This gigantic city, 1500 miles in height, length and width (which means it could be either pyramid or cube shaped) will be the eternal destination for the Saints and will be beautiful beyond description.

It seems as if God has to demonstrate to the Saints one last time before they reach their eternal destination, the consequences of Satan's original sins of pride and rebellion from which all sin is derived. God is not going to allow another Satan to arise ever again. After all, before Satan sinned he was Lucifer, the most beautiful angel and chief worshipper of the Almighty. God is returning His creation to the perfect state in which it existed before the rebellion of Satan and his angels and the fall of man. Christ died on the cross once and for all. Any lessons or demonstrations of God's power during the Millennium and how He deals with Satan's final rebellion must surely therefore be for the instruction of the **Saints**, not for the unbelieving world. The unbelieving world is to be consigned to the lake of fire together with Satan and all his host. Escape is impossible, they are consigned there for eternity. There is no redemption, no possible rehabilitation, God has finished His dealings with them.

There is to be eternal separation from God and the Saints, those whose names are not in the Book of Life will never be referred to again, it will be as if they had never existed. There is nothing further that they should learn. It is a terrible judgement and a dramatic contrast to the amazing grace and mercy the Lord has shown to the Saints.

'What shall we say then? Is there unrighteousness with God? Certainly not! For He says to Moses, "I will have mercy on whomever I will have mercy, and I will have compassion on whomever I will have compassion." So then it is not of him who wills, nor of him who runs, but of God who shows mercy. For the Scripture says to Pharaoh, "Even for this same purpose I have raised you up, that I may show My power in you, and that My name may be declared in all the earth." Therefore He has mercy on whom He wills, and whom He wills He hardens. You will say to me then, "Why does He still find fault? For who has resisted His will?" But indeed, O man, who are you to reply against God? Will the thing

formed say to him who formed it, "Why have you made me like this?" Does not the potter have power over the clay, from the same lump to make one vessel for honour and another for dishonour? What if God, wanting to show His wrath and to make His power known, endured with much longsuffering the vessels of wrath prepared for destruction, and that He might make known the riches of His glory on the vessels of mercy, which He had prepared beforehand for glory, even us whom He called, not of the Jews only, but also of the Gentiles?'

(Romans 9:14–24)

APPENDICES

Appendix A

The Ten Kingdoms
by Malcolm

There has been much speculation in many books on the subject of the end-time as to which countries will constitute the ten kingdoms, mentioned in Daniel and Revelation. These are the kingdoms of the ten kings of the earth who, *'give their power and authority to the beast'* (Revelation 17:13).

Most commentators have interpreted the scriptures and defined these kingdoms as being a collection of European nations arising out of the cultural inheritance of the old Roman Empire. Contenders have been variously thought to be:

- **The United Nations** – but they have too many nations in the wrong part of the world to be seriously considered.

- **Ten regions of a one-world government** – but they have same problem as the United Nations.

- **The Common Market or European Union** – the European Union could be a candidate for the ten kingdoms, after all, they have many members who were in the past, part of the Roman Empire; but they too have too many members, with several more countries applying for membership.

We do not know who these 'ten kings' (nations) might be, but the following information is worthy of interest.

The Western European Union

Not many people have heard of The Western European Union (WEU). It is a purely military force and originated as the Brussels Treaty Organization established under the Treaty of Brussels signed by Great Britain, France, Belgium, Luxembourg, and The Netherlands in 1948. (The same year that Israel became a nation!)

In 1954 West Germany and Italy were admitted. However because of the establishment of NATO and the Council of Europe the WEU became defunct.

In 1984 the WEU was reactivated with members committed to a common policy on defence and security with a purely European identity separate from and outside NATO.

Two more countries, Portugal and Spain, were admitted as members in 1988. In the Petersburg declaration in 1992 it was agreed to assign troops to WEU authority for 'peace-making' operations in Europe.

In 1992, Iceland, Norway, Turkey, Ireland and Denmark became associate members. In 1994, Estonia, Latvia, Lithuania, Poland, Czech Republic, Slovak Republic, Hungary, Romania and Bulgaria all became associate partners.

The WEU was involved in joint actions in the Gulf War and currently operates a naval patrol force in the Adriatic, the River Danube, and a police force in Mostar in the former Yugoslavia.

It has a 'Eurocorps' force answerable only to the WEU, consisting of 51,000 troops made up of French, German, Belgian, Luxembourg and Spanish forces. Only recently in 1995, with the admittance of Greece, the original nine full members became **ten**.

1. Great Britain
2. France
3. Belgium
4. Luxembourg
5. The Netherlands
6. West Germany
7. Italy
8. Portugal
9. Spain
10. Greece

Appendix B

The Doomsday Asteroid
by Malcolm

'The first angel sounded: And hail and fire followed, mingled with blood, and they were thrown to the earth; and a third of the trees were burnt up, and all green grass was burned up.'
(Revelation 8:7)

*'Then the second angel sounded: And something like **a great mountain** burning with fire was thrown into the sea, and a third of the sea became blood; and a third of the living creatures in the sea died, and a third of the ships were destroyed.'* (Revelation 8:8–9)

*'Then the third angel sounded: And **a great star** fell from heaven, burning like a torch, and it fell on a third of the rivers and on the springs of water.'* (Revelation 8:10)

*'And the name of the **star** is Wormwood; and a third of the waters became wormwood; and many men died from the water, because it was made bitter.* (Revelation 8:11)

These passages seem to be descriptions of a large Asteroid, or its fragments, colliding with our own planet. Could this be possible? Are there any Asteroids, Comets or Meteors out in our Solar System, hurtling toward Earth that these scriptures could be predicting? Could there be any connection with the date – 2004 and the possible Return of the Lord Jesus Christ?

On the 20th November 1995, BBC Television broadcast a Horizon Programme entitled, *Doomsday Asteroid Update.* The following information has been extracted from the original script and the British Broadcasting Corporation has given its permission for its publication in this book.

'When the Shoemaker-Levy comet collided with the planet Jupiter in July 1994, it came as almost a complete surprise to astronomers who had detected its presence only some fifteen months previously.

Scientists were able to observe at first-hand the effects of this comet striking Jupiter and calculate the devastation if such a visitation were to occur on the Earth. Jupiter's enormous gravitational pull ripped the comet into 21 huge pieces which proceeded to plunge through the giant planet's atmosphere at enormous speed.

Gene Shoemaker predicted the huge destructive potential of these impacts and many experts thought that he was exaggerating.

Keith Noll said, "We're gonna see nothing because these things are big piles of stuff with the consistency of cigarette ash."

English Astronomer, Patrick Moore said, "Astronomy attracts cranks and crackpots in the same way a jam-jar attracts wasps. The effect on Jupiter is going to be absolutely minimal. Jupiter is a vast planet – a comet a very lightweight thing. As I've said, you might as well try to stop a charging rhinoceros by throwing a baked bean at it."

On the 16th July 1994, the first fragment of Comet Shoemaker-Levy, collided with Jupiter. The cloud of debris spread out for thousands of miles and was over 1000 miles high. The following day the dustcloud had increased to the size of the Earth. The third fragment caused a fireball hotter than 20,000 degrees Celsius to erupt thousands of kilometres out into space before being dragged back down to the surface of the planet by the force of gravity.

Jupiter is 300 times larger than the earth. If just one of those fragments had struck Earth the results would have been devastating. There are some 150 large meteor craters around the world including the Yucatan crater in Mexico, Central

America, which is thought to have caused the mass extinction of half of the species all over the world including the dinosaurs. The last major comet impact experienced on earth was in 1908, in Siberia, when a fireball exploded in the air before it hit the ground. Fortunately it was in an unpopulated area, but it still destroyed hundreds of miles of forest.

Sensors located in satellites orbiting the earth regularly detect meteors detonating as they burn up in the earth's outer atmosphere. In 1991 a 10 kilotonne explosion was detected over the Pacific ocean. A 10 kilometre crater would require the energy equivalent of all the nuclear weapons in the world detonating simultaneously – 10,000 megatons makes a 10 kilometre crater. Recently geologists found tell-tale signs beneath the Gulf of Mexico of a 65 million year old crater almost 200 kilometres across.

Scientists have discovered about 2000 of these asteroids larger than 1 kilometre across, a few hundred thousand larger than 100 metres and around 150 million larger than 10 metres. None of which were known until recently.

Gene Shoemaker and his team systematically surveyed the space near the Earth for Earth-crossing bodies – asteroids and comets that could hit the Earth. The rocks he saw were tiny by astronomical standards, but the more Shoemaker looked, the more he saw. Despite their faint image, these were not pebbles.

These streaks represented huge mountains of rock weighing millions of tons all with the potential to hit Earth. While for decades astronomers had been probing the galaxies beyond our solar system, they had ignored what was right under our noses.

Essentially there are two catastrophic machines in the Solar System which are directing missiles at us.

One of them is the asteroid belt, which is regularly perturbed by Jupiter in its orbit close to the asteroid belt. The other one is the so-called Oort Cloud which is perturbed by the galactic environment. Both these sets of perturbations result in asteroids or comets being deflected from their normal places into the centre of the Solar System, where they may be trapped through further interactions with the circulating planets and it is the ones that are trapped that are potentially dangerous. The Earth is a kind of target amongst all these bodies milling around which have come from places further out in the Solar System. Over a certain size, the atmosphere no longer shields the Earth's surface from these rocks.

Imagine for a moment if instead of these objects being not visible to the naked eye they were suddenly made visible. Suppose that there was a button you could push and you could light up all the Earth-crossing asteroids in the sky and you went outside at night. Instead of being able to see a few thousand bright stars, the sky would be filled with millions of these objects, all of which are capable of colliding with the Earth, and all of which are moving on slightly different courses through the sky at different rates.

The number of Astronomers involved worldwide, in looking for Earth-threatening, or "Doomsday" asteroids as they are nick-named, is less than the staff of something like a high street McDonalds restaurant. In 1990 a group of independent scientists decided to lobby the US Government Space Sub-Committee, suggesting that we ought to have some plan to cope with impacts. Their move was prompted by the fact that a year before, a rock the size of an aircraft carrier, passed close to the earth and was only spotted after it had gone by.

Any object larger than 1 kilometre across is big enough to cause a mass extinction. These meteors that could kill a quarter of the earth's population arrive on earth quite infrequently, every few million years or so. But they are almost impossible to detect until the very last few months until impact, because they travel on erratic trajectories, constantly being pulled into new orbits as they pass close to large planets. A couple of years ago an Astronomer named Steve Ostro pinpointed one of these large asteroids with a radio telescope.

Toutatis, as it is known, is some four and a half kilometres long and two kilometres wide. This huge mountain will come the closest to earth of any known asteroid – in the year **2004.'**

Latest Asteroid update

Since writing this chapter, but before the publication of this book the following are extracts of an article published in the *London Times* on 30th November 1996.

> 'One of the most unusual objects in the solar system passes within 3.3 million miles of the earth today. The closest approach corresponds to about 14 times the distance from the Earth to the Moon ... The rocky body's strange traits are believed to be the result of a history of violent collisions. Toutatis may have the most chaotic orbit studied to date, a consequence of the asteroid's frequent close approaches to earth ... "Toutatis, if it landed on the Earth would have the force of exploding the entire world's nuclear arsenal," added Dr Willstrop of Cambridge University's Institute of Astronomy ... **On September 29th, 2004**, Toutatis will pass four lunar distances from Earth (943,000 miles), the closest approach of any known asteroid or comet between now and 2060.'

On 10th November 1996 the Sunday edition the *London Times* published an article on how the mystery of the sudden extinction of the dinosaurs may have been caused by a giant Asteroid colliding with the Earth some 65 million years ago.

> 'In addition to cutting out the sunlight, the impact of the asteroid probably ejected massive quantities of acidic particles that fell as rain turning the oceans acidic ... The asteroid would have smashed through the atmosphere and hit Earth in a fraction of a second, vaporising on impact. Earthquakes would have registered 12 on the Richter scale, 1000 times bigger than the severest earthquakes today.'

(See Appendix D)

Appendix C

The Scrolls Containing the
Seven Seals – Trumpets – Bowls
by Malcolm

T he series of events marked by the seven Seals, seven
Trumpets and seven Bowls of Revelation need to be
viewed in their entirety in order to gain an understanding of
the unfolding of events they describe. There is a variety
of opinion and interpretation on the order of the opening of
the seals and the juxtaposition of trumpets and bowls.

Are they consecutive, concurrent or a mixture of the
two?

In our opinion:

1. The First seal reveals the Anti-Christ.
2. The Second seal reveals the Wars on Earth which follow.
3. The Third seal reveals widespread Famine.
4. The Fourth seal reveals widespread Death on Earth.
5. The Fifth seal reveals Believers persecuted on Earth.
6. The Sixth seal reveals the Wrath of God **about** to be
    poured out.

The Seven trumpets announce the Seven bowls and each
is coupled with its opposite number thus:

1. *First Trumpet* – hail, fire and blood strike the earth's
    landmass.
    First Bowl – poured out on earth, sores on flesh with
    mark of the beast.

2. *Second Trumpet* – great mountain burning with fire (a piece of Asteroid?) hits the Sea; one third of living creatures in the sea die.
    Second Bowl – sea turns to blood, every living creature in the sea dies.
3. *Third Trumpet* – great star burning like a torch (a second piece of Asteroid?) hits the land; one third of fresh water polluted.
    Third Bowl – rivers and springs become blood (polluted).
4. *Fourth Trumpet* – Sun, Moon and Stars, darkened – daylight hours reduced.
    Fourth Bowl – protection from Ultra Violet Sunlight reduced, men scorched.
5. *Fifth Trumpet* – Demons released torture mankind, Sun and Air darkened.
    Fifth Bowl – Mankind tortured by pain and sores – Darkness on earth.
6. *Sixth Trumpet* – third of Mankind killed in war in Euphrates area.
    Sixth Bowl – Euphrates river dammed, armies gather together in Armageddon.

Immediately before the Seventh Seal – Reference is made here to Sealed 144,000 of Israel **and** the Great Multitude **appearing** in Heaven.

Immediately before the Seventh Trumpet – Reference is made to '**Mystery of God**' being '**finished**' at the sounding of seventh angel.

Immediately before the Seventh Bowl – Reference is made to Christ's return,

> *'Behold, I am coming as a thief. Blessed is he who watches and keeps his garments, lest he walk naked and they see his shame.'*

As we have stated previously we believe these three references describe the **Rapture of the Saints and the Second Coming of the Lord**, occurring at this point.

7. *Seventh Seal* – describes God's wrath **being** poured out. Noises, thunderings, lightnings and an earthquake.

Seventh Trump – Kingdom Proclaimed, announcement of God's wrath – lightnings, noises, thunderings, earthquake and great hail.

Seventh Bowl – Earth utterly shaken, announcement from heaven saying, *'It is done!'*, thunderings, lightnings, noises, and the **greatest earthquake** of all time.

The sequence of events may be represented thus:

Seals	1 2 3 4 5 6	7
Trumpets		{1 2 3 4 5 6 7}
Bowls		{1 2 3 4 5 6 7}

(It may be purely coincidental but there are three series of six events, 666 (the number of the beast or the anti-christ), each capped with a common seventh event (incorporating as we believe, the Rapture and the Second Coming), or 777 which is the number of perfection and the number of God.)

At the sounding of the Seventh trumpet Jesus returns to earth for and with the saints and defeats the anti-christ, the beast and the kings of the earth at Armageddon. Satan is then bound in the bottomless pit for 1000 years. The saints then reign with Christ on earth for 1000 years.

It is **not** our intention to attempt to predict when all this will happen or to 'set dates'.

Scripture says clearly that:

> *'But of that day and hour no one knows, no, not even the angels of heaven, but My Father only.'*   (Matthew 24:36)

However, we believe it interesting to say the least, that several indicators point to a cumulation of events taking place, just after the end of this century. The world at large, including many Christians, scoff at the notion, that the Lord might return soon. Others say that the year 2000 is an obvious choice, but for the reasons we give below, we suspect it might be a little later than that.

1.   Scripture states that with the Lord a day is as a 1000 years and a 1000 years as one day. Some Bible Commentators believe that this arithmetic goes as follows:

From Adam to Abraham	2000 years (2 days)
From Abraham to Christ	2000 years (2 days)
From Christ's death (held by many Bible scholars to have occurred around 33.25 AD) to the second advent	**2000 years (2 days)**
Total	<u>6000</u> years (6 days)
The Millennium after the return of Jesus	**1000 years (1 day)**

This would mean that Jesus would return 2000 years after his crucifixion.

*'and that He was buried, and that He rose again the **third day** according to the Scriptures.'*
(1 Corinthians 15:4)

2. If Jesus was crucified in the month of April at the age of 33 and returned to earth 2000 years later, then using the Jewish prophetic/lunar year of the Book of Daniel, which had 30 days to a month, the following calculation converts 2000 Jewish prophetic/lunar years to our own solar years, each of 365.24 days:

    $2000 \times 360 \div 365.24 = 1971.31$ solar years
    33.25 AD + 1971.31 years
    = 2004.56 AD
    = the dawn of the third day

The Millennium is also known as the thousand years of peace, or the Day of the Lord. God made the Heavens and the earth in six days and rested on the seventh or Sabbath day. In the past many have tried to predict the date of the second coming of the Lord. 1884, 1918, 1928, 1933, 1948, 1984 were some of the dates that were suggested. They were obviously wrong.

Will it be 2004.56? No-one knows but the Father!

The date 2004.56 could correspond to the 23rd day of July 2005. The book of Daniel describes the Great tribulation as lasting 1260 days. A further 30 and 45 days are added to describe 1290 and 1335 day periods.

> *'Blessed is he who waits and comes to the one thousand three hundred and thirty five days. But you go your way till the end; for you shall rest, and will arise to your inheritance at the end of the days.'*
>
> (Daniel 12:12–13)

3. Jesus' Second coming is described in scripture as happening, *'after the tribulation of those days...'*

   30 days plus 45 days (75 days) from the 23rd July on a Jewish 30-day month brings us into the month of October.

   The Jewish 'Feast of Trumpets' is a prophetic feast and refers to the future re-gathering of Israel and is celebrated on the 1st day of the month of Tishri (September/October).

> *'And you will be gathered one by one.*
> *O you children of Israel.*
> *So it shall be in that day*
> *That the great trumpet will be blown.'*
>
> (Isaiah 27:12–13)

> *'And He will send His angels with a great sound of a trumpet, and they will gather together His elect from the four winds, from one end of heaven to the other.'*
>
> (Matthew 24:31)

The 'Feast of Atonement' refers to the future repentance of Israel after their re-gathering and is held on the 10th of Tishri (September/October).

> *'Come, let us return to the LORD,*
> *For He has torn, but He will Heal us;*
> *He has stricken, but He will bind us up.*
> *After two days He will revive us;*
> *On the third day He will raise us up,*
> *That we may live in His sight.'*
>
> (Hosea 6:1–2)

The 'Feast of Tabernacles' is a prophetic feast and looks forward to the restoration of the Kingdom of Israel after her regathering and becomes a memorial not only for Israel but for all nations and begins on the 15th day of Tishri (September/October).

> *'And I heard a loud voice from heaven saying, "Behold, the tabernacle of God is with men, and He will dwell with them, and they shall be His people, and God Himself will be with them and be their God." '*   (Revelation 21:3)

Having said all this, we would be extremely foolish to claim that Jesus is certain to return during the year 2005. However we would say that Jesus **has** to return at some time and there **will** be a final generation. We would not be at all surprised if it were **ours**.

Appendix D

Signs of the Times and the End of the Age
by Malcolm

'Now as He sat on the Mount of Olives, the disciples came to Him privately, saying, "Tell us, when will these things be? And what will be the sign of Your coming and of the end of the age?" And Jesus answered them and said to them, "Take heed that no-one deceives you. For many will come in My name, saying, 'I am the Christ,' and will deceive many. And you will hear of wars and rumours of wars. See that you are not troubled; for all these things must come to pass, but the end is not yet. For nation will rise against nation, and kingdom against kingdom. And there will be famines, pestilences, and earthquakes in various places. All these are the beginning of sorrows."' (Matthew 24:3–8)

'And there will be great earthquakes in various places, and famines and pestilences; and there will be fearful sights and great signs from heaven.' (Luke 21:11)

1. 'Many will come in my name, saying, "I am the Christ."'

There have been many false Messiah's. One of the most recent, David Koresh in Waco Texas, convinced his deluded followers that he was the Christ with tragic consequences.

2. *'You will hear of wars and rumours of wars'*

There are currently over 200 armed conflicts worldwide.

3.*'Famines'*

Famines are not new. There have been famines in the past; many are described in the Old Testament, but never before in history has there been such famine in the world as there is right now. Today the World Watch Institute estimates that 80,000 people die per hour, 24 hours per day from starvation. 786 million people are experiencing acute or chronic hunger with a further 1000 million people seriously malnutritioned.

The Institute publishes figures that show that food production worldwide reached maximum levels in the 1980s. The figures for 1994 show that we are producing 8 per cent less food now.

The Earth has never experienced these levels of famine before.

4. *'Pestilences'*

New strains of TB are sweeping Russia and Eastern Europe. A recent case in London confirmed in March 1995 marks the arrival of this strain in the UK. These new strains are totally resistant to all current known antibiotics.

In 1994 the CIA warned the US government that if the spread of AIDS in Africa continued at its present rate, 75 percent of the population south of the Sahara (i.e. 250 million people) could contract AIDS and die by the year 2000. In Zimbabwe, 7 percent of blood donors were shown to have AIDS. Twelve months later the figure had risen to 47 percent.

The figures for Asia and India are equally bad. In Asia during 1987 there was 1 confirmed case of AIDS. In 1995 there were more than 3 million cases.

- Over 96% of all prostitutes in Thailand have AIDS
- Over 60% of all prostitutes in India have AIDS
- Over 60% of all prostitutes in Paris have AIDS

AIDS is the first 100 percent fatal epidemic known to

man, no-one has recovered after contracting full-blown AIDS.

At the time of writing this section of our book, BSE or 'Mad Cow' disease has afflicted the British Beef Industry. The British government is under pressure from the European Union to destroy and incinerate 4.5 million cattle in the UK. Scientists have discovered that there may be a link between BSE in cattle and CJD a fatal brain infection in humans.

Neither BSE nor CJD have any known cure at present. The disease in cattle is thought to have been caused by the feeding of bovine offal, bone and blood meal to cattle. In fact, cattle being made to feed on themselves. Cows are herbivores and are just not designed to eat meat, let alone each other.

5. *'Fearful sights and great signs from heaven'*

The 'first heaven' is defined as 'the air around us' – the atmosphere, the skies where the clouds gather. Storms, thunder and lightning are greater than ever before. The Ozone layer and the Equatorial rainforests are currently being destroyed at an incredible rate. Giant holes measuring over 9 million square miles have been detected in the Ozone layer in the Southern hemisphere. This hole is equal to the size of Europe. Cattle in Chile are being blinded and dying. The maximum period that a human being may be exposed there without harm is 30 minutes.

Recent readings from the Total Ozone Mapping Spectrometer aboard NASA's Nimbus-7 satellite show that between the 1970s and 1990s radiation from the sun has increased by an average of 7% per decade, with 10% per decade being recorded for South America. NASA is alarmed because the increase is taking place at middle latitudes including Europe and Russia where the majority of the planet's population lives. Other scientists report that 3 percent of the ozone protective layer has already been destroyed. They calculate that at 15 per cent millions will die of cancer.

80,000 square miles of rain forest, the 'lungs' of the planet are destroyed each year. The area of devastation is equivalent in size to the country of Austria. This destruction involving the burning of large areas of rain forest releases large amounts of carbon dioxide into the atmosphere, leading to a greenhouse effect on the world's climate. During the last twenty three years the earth's average temperature has risen steadily, causing partial melting of the Polar Ice caps, leading to widespread coastal flooding in the Northern Hemisphere.

All these activities have caused turbulent weather patterns. New extremes of weather are being experienced worldwide and records are being continually broken. A weather pattern in Central America named 'El Niño' (Spanish for 'the Christ Child'), is caused by warming waters in the South Pacific and is normally of 12 to 18 months duration. Gerald Bell, a meteorologist with the National Oceanic and Atmospheric Administration confirms the current one began in 1989 and is the longest on record. He attributes extraordinary hurricanes originating in the South Pacific and the 1993 Mid-West flooding to this continuing weather pattern.

In 1993 the volcano Mount Pinatubo in the Philippines erupted with the equivalent power of one nuclear bomb exploding every second for twenty-four hours and spewed out huge quantities of sulphur dioxide high up into the atmosphere. Scientists calculate that the resultant cloud deflected 3 per cent of the sun's rays away from the earth. The following year South Africa had its worst drought in 100 years. In 1984 in the state of California, seismologists of the US Geological Survey detected a Magma (Molten Rock) intrusion measuring some 100 sq. miles wide, centred on the dormant volcano Mount Mammoth in the Long Valley Caldera, rising at the rate of 2 inches per annum. This may not sound very much but it is equivalent in geological terms to a Saturn V rocket leaving the launch pad. Some experts calculate at this rate the volcano is likely to erupt sometime within twenty years – by the year 2004. They estimate that it will spew out 140 cubic miles of ash (by comparison, Mount St. Helens in 1980 produced a quarter of a cubic mile of ash). The resultant fall out from this eruption is predicted to blanket everything within 75 miles in 3 feet of ash.

6. 'Earthquakes'

The following information is based on data supplied by the US Geological Survey, on Earthquakes of 6.0 or greater occurring worldwide since 1890 (see Figure 2).

1890–1899	219 earthquakes
1900–1909	545 earthquakes
1910–1919	753 earthquakes
1920–1929	1043 earthquakes
1930–1939	1961 earthquakes
1940–1949	1591 earthquakes
1950–1959	2358 earthquakes
1960–1969	2052 earthquakes
1970–1979	1816 earthquakes
1980–1989	1449 earthquakes
1990–1995	916 earthquakes

The US GS explains that the increase could be due to improvements in detection methods and seismic equipment, nevertheless they cannot rule out the fact that it could be due to the fact that great earthquakes are increasing on a global scale. An earthquake measuring 6.8 occurred on 17th January 1994, in North Ridge, USA causing 20 billion dollars worth of damage. Earthquakes measuring 8.0 or greater have previously occurred in the USA in remote areas such as Alaska. An 8.0 is 85 times more powerful than a 6.8. It is difficult to even hazard a guess at the damage something that big would inflict in a heavily populated area. Jesus said, *'all these things must come to pass.'*

As we race towards the year 2000, 'Millennium Fever' will undoubtedly break out everywhere. Many books will appear on the subject of 'the end of the world' and as we have already stated, most people, including many Christians, will scoff at the notion that the Lord's return may be imminent. However they may do well to consider the 'Signs of the Times'. Never before in the history of the planet have all these conditions occurred on earth, as prophesied by Jesus, racing towards a climax, as indeed they are right now.

Jesus said, *'The end is not yet.'*

But Margaret and I believe we are very close! Figure 2

Figure 2   Heading for the Big One: *Increase in the average number of Major Global Earthquakes of 6.0 or greater on the Richter Scale recorded per year since 1890.*

graphically shows the inevitable march towards the **'great and mighty earthquake'** of Revelation 16:18 – **'such as had not occurred since men were on the earth'!**

> *'For the earnest expectation of the creation eagerly awaits for the revealing of the sons of God. For the creation was subjected to futility, not willingly, but because of Him who subjected it in hope; because the creation itself also will be delivered from the bondage of corruption into the glorious liberty of the children of God. For we know that the whole creation groans and labours with birth pangs together until now.'*   (Romans 8:19–22)

In 1948 the State of Israel came into existence:

> *'So you also, when you see all these things know that it is near, at the very doors. "Assuredly, I say to you this generation will by no means pass away till all these things are fulfilled."'* (Matthew 24:33–34)

Is ours the generation that will see all these things fulfilled and the return of the Lord Jesus Christ?

Epilogue

If you are not a believer in, or follower of Jesus Christ and you have managed to stay with this book right through until this page – then well done!

We doubt whether we could have read this far ourselves, before we became born again Christians. Margaret and I will now tell you a true fact and ask you a question.

True fact

Everyone who has ever lived will receive immortality at either the first or second resurrection. Settle it in your heart right now, you **will** exist forever.

Question

The question for you to answer is: **Where do you want to spend your eternal existence?**

God has given Mankind free choice, so the choice is yours.

You can choose consignment to the lake of fire and spend your eternal existence in torment with Satan, the rebellious angels and all unbelievers – or you can have eternal life with Jesus in Glory with the Saints.

If you want to choose Jesus, then pray out loud this short prayer right now.

Lord Jesus, I come to You now as I am.
I am sorry for the sin in my life.
I turn away from my sins right now.
I believe that You are the risen Son
   of the living God and that You died for me that
   I might enter Your Kingdom and
   have Eternal Life through Your shed blood.
Please forgive me and accept me as one
   of Your own.
Thank You Lord.
Amen.

Tell someone what you have just prayed and get yourself into a Spirit-filled church or Christian fellowship as soon as possible.

Welcome into the Kingdom of God.

If you did not feel that you could pray this prayer – well that's your choice. But do not forget the things you have read in this book. There may well soon come a time when you will be desperate enough, as we were, to call upon the Lord for His Salvation.

He always hears and He is always ready to bring you too:

'Out of Darkness into His Marvellous Light.'